Edmund Burke, Cornelius Beach Bradley

Conciliation with the colonies

Edmund Burke, Cornelius Beach Bradley

Conciliation with the colonies

ISBN/EAN: 9783337150044

Printed in Europe, USA, Canada, Australia, Japan

Cover: Foto ©ninafisch / pixelio.de

More available books at **www.hansebooks.com**

The Academy Series of English Classics

BURKE

CONCILIATION WITH THE COLONIES

EDITED BY

CORNELIUS BEACH BRADLEY

PROFESSOR OF RHETORIC IN THE UNIVERSITY
OF CALIFORNIA

Boston
ALLYN AND BACON

PUBLISHERS' NOTE.

This book contains portions of a larger volume prepared by the same editor. The page numbers have not been changed, and the breaks in the paging occur where matter of the larger volume has been omitted.

All the works in *The Academy Series of English Classics* are given without abbreviation.

EDMUND BURKE.

ON MOVING HIS
RESOLUTIONS FOR CONCILIATION WITH THE COLONIES.
HOUSE OF COMMONS, MARCH 22, 1775.

I HOPE, Sir, that notwithstanding the austerity of the Chair, your good nature will incline you to some degree of indulgence towards human frailty. You will not think it unnatural that those who have an object depending, which strongly engages their hopes and fears, should be somewhat inclined to superstition. As I came into the House full of anxiety about the event of my motion, I found, to my infinite surprise, that the grand penal bill, by which we had passed sentence on the trade and sustenance of America, is to be returned to us from the other House. I do confess I could not help looking on this event as a fortunate omen. I look upon it as a sort of providential favor, by which we are put once more in possession of our deliberative capacity upon a business so very questionable in its nature, so very uncertain in its issue. By the return of this bill, which seemed to have taken its flight forever, we are at this very instant nearly as free to choose a plan for our American Government as we were on the first day of the session. If, Sir, we incline to the side of conciliation, we are not at all embarrassed (unless we please to make ourselves so) by any incongruous mixture of coercion and restraint.

drawing out something like a platform of the ground which might be laid for future and permanent tranquillity.

I felt the truth of what my honorable friend represented; but I felt my situation too. His application might have been made with far greater propriety to many other gentlemen. No man was indeed ever better disposed, or worse qualified, for such an undertaking than myself. Though I gave so far in to his opinion that I immediately threw my thoughts into a sort of Parliamentary form. I was by no means equally ready to produce them. It generally argues some degree of natural impotence of mind, or some want of knowledge of the world, to hazard plans of government except from a seat of authority. Propositions are made, not only ineffectually, but somewhat disreputably, when the minds of men are not properly disposed for their reception; and, for my part, I am not ambitious of ridicule — not absolutely a candidate for disgrace.

Besides, Sir, to speak the plain truth, I have in general no very exalted opinion of the virtue of paper government; nor of any politics in which the plan is to be wholly separated from the execution. But when I saw that anger and violence prevailed every day more and more, and that things were hastening towards an incurable alienation of our Colonies, I confess my caution gave way. I felt this as one of those few moments in which decorum yields to a higher duty. Public calamity is a mighty leveller; and there are occasions when any, even the slightest, chance of doing good must be laid hold on, even by the most inconsiderable person.

To restore order and repose to an empire so great and so distracted as ours, is, merely in the attempt, an undertaking that would ennoble the flights of the highest genius, and obtain pardon for the efforts of the meanest understanding. Struggling a good while with these thoughts, by degrees I felt myself more firm. I derived, at length, some confidence from what in other circumstances usually produces timidity. I grew less anxious, even from the idea of my own insignificance. For, judging of what you are by what you ought to be, I persuaded myself that you would not reject a reasonable proposition because it had nothing but its reason to recommend it. On the other hand, being totally destitute of all shadow of influence, natural or adventitious, I was very sure that, if my proposition were futile or dangerous — if it were weakly conceived, or improperly timed — there was nothing exterior to it of power to awe, dazzle, or delude you. You will see it just as it is; and you will treat it just as it deserves.

The proposition is peace. Not peace through the medium of war; not peace to be hunted through the labyrinth of intricate and endless negotiations; not peace to arise out of universal discord fomented, from principle, in all parts of the Empire; not peace to depend on the juridical determination of perplexing questions, or the precise marking the shadowy boundaries of a complex government. It is simple peace; sought in its natural course, and in its ordinary haunts. It is peace sought in the spirit of peace, and laid in principles purely pacific. I propose, by removing the ground of the difference, and by restoring the former unsuspecting confidence of the Colonies in the Mother Country, to give permanent satisfaction to your people; and (far from a scheme of ruling by discord) to reconcile them to each other in the same act and by the bond of the very same interest which reconciles them to British government.

My idea is nothing more. Refined policy ever has been the parent of confusion; and ever will be so, as long as the world endures. Plain good intention, which is as easily discovered at the first view as fraud is surely detected at last, is, let me say, of no mean force in the government of mankind. Genuine simplicity of heart is an healing and cementing principle. My plan, therefore, being formed upon the most simple grounds imaginable, may disappoint some people when they hear it. It has nothing to recommend it to the pruriency of curious ears. There is nothing at all new and captivating in it. It has nothing of the splendor of the project which has been lately laid upon your table by the noble lord in the blue ribbon. It does not propose to fill your lobby with squabbling Colony agents, who will require the interposition of your mace, at every instant, to keep the peace amongst them. It does not institute a magnificent auction of finance, where captivated provinces come to general ransom by bidding against each other, until you knock down the hammer, and determine a proportion of payments beyond all the powers of algebra to equalize and settle.

The plan which I shall presume to suggest derives, however, one great advantage from the proposition and registry of that noble lord's project. The idea of conciliation is admissible. First, the House, in accepting the resolution moved by the noble lord, has admitted, notwithstanding the menacing front of our address, notwithstanding our heavy bills of pains and penalties — that we do not think ourselves precluded from all ideas of free grace and bounty.

The House has gone farther; it has declared conciliation admissible, previous to any submission on the part of America. It has even shot a good deal beyond that mark, and has admitted that the complaints of our former mode of exerting the right of taxation were not wholly unfounded. That right thus exerted is allowed to have something reprehensible in it, something unwise, or something grievous; since, in the midst of our heat and resentment, we, of ourselves, have proposed a capital alteration; and in order to get rid of what seemed so very exceptionable, have instituted a mode that is altogether new; one that is, indeed, wholly alien from all the ancient methods and forms of Parliament.

The principle of this proceeding is large enough for my purpose. The means proposed by the noble lord for carrying his ideas into execution, I think, indeed, are very indifferently suited to the end; and this I shall endeavor to show you before I sit down. But, for the present, I take my ground on the admitted principle. I mean to give peace. Peace implies reconciliation; and where there has been a material dispute, reconciliation does in a manner always imply concession on the one part or on the other. In this state of things I make no difficulty in affirming that the proposal ought to originate, from us. Great and acknowledged force is not impaired, either in effect or in opinion, by an unwillingness to exert itself. The superior power may offer peace with honor and with safety. Such an offer from such a power will be attributed to magnanimity. But the concessions of the weak are the concessions of fear. When such a one is disarmed, he is wholly at the mercy of his superior; and he loses forever that time and those chances, which, as they happen to all men, are the strength and resources of all inferior power.

The capital leading questions on which you must this day decide are these two: First, whether you ought to concede; and secondly, what your concession ought to be. On the first of these questions we have gained, as I have just taken the liberty of observing to you, some ground. But I am sensible that a good deal more is still to be done. Indeed, Sir, to enable us to determine both on the one and the other of these great questions with a firm and precise judgment, I think it may be necessary to consider distinctly the true nature and the peculiar circumstances of the object which we have before us; because after all our struggle, whether we will or not, we must govern America according to that nature and to those circumstances, and not according to our own imaginations, nor according to abstract ideas of right — by no means according to mere general theories of government, the resort to which appears to me, in our present situation, no better than arrant trifling. I shall therefore endeavor, with your leave, to lay before you some of the most material of these circumstances in as full and as clear a manner as I am able to state them.

The first thing that we have to consider with regard to the nature of the object is — the number of people in the Colonies. I have taken for some years a good deal of pains on that point. I can by no calculation justify myself in placing the number below two millions of inhabitants of our own European blood and color, besides at least five hundred thousand others, who form no inconsiderable part of the strength and opulence of the whole. This, Sir, is, I believe, about the true number. There is no occasion to exaggerate where plain truth is of so much weight and importance. But whether I put the present numbers too high or too low is a matter of little moment. Such is the strength with which population shoots in that part of the world, that, state the numbers as high as we will, whilst the dispute continues, the exaggeration ends. Whilst we are discussing any given magnitude, they are grown to it. Whilst we spend our time in deliberating on the mode of governing two millions, we shall find we have millions more to manage. Your children do not grow faster from infancy to manhood than they spread from families to communities, and from villages to nations.

I put this consideration of the present and the growing numbers in the front of our deliberation, because, Sir, this consideration will make it evident to a blunter discernment than yours, that no partial, narrow, contracted, pinched, occasional system will be at all suitable to such an object. It will show you that it is not to be considered as one of those *minima* which are out of the eye and consideration of the law; not a paltry excrescence of the state; not a mean dependant, who may be neglected with little damage and provoked with little danger. It will prove that some degree of care and caution is required in the handling such an object; it will show that you ought not, in reason, to trifle with so large a mass of the interests and feelings of the human race. You could at no time do so without guilt; and be assured you will not be able to do it long with impunity.

But the population of this country, the great and growing population, though a very important consideration, will lose much of its weight if not combined with other circumstances. The commerce of your Colonies is out of all proportion beyond the numbers of the people. This ground of their commerce indeed has been trod some days ago, and with great ability, by a distinguished person at your bar. This gentleman, after thirty-five years — it is so long since he first appeared at the same place to plead for the commerce of Great Britain — has come again before you to plead the same cause, without any other effect of time, than that to the fire of imagination and extent of erudition which even then marked him as one of the first literary characters of his age, he has added a consummate knowledge in the commercial interest of his country, formed by a long course of enlightened and discriminating experience.

Sir, I should be inexcusable in coming after such a person with any detail, if a great part of the members who now fill the House had not the misfortune to be absent when he appeared at your bar. Besides, Sir, I propose to take the matter at periods of time somewhat different from his. There is, if I mistake not, a point of view from whence, if you will look at the subject, it is impossible that it should not make an impression upon you.

I have in my hand two accounts; one a comparative state of the export trade of England to its Colonies, as it stood in the year 1704, and as it stood in the year 1772; the other a state of the export trade of this country to its Colonies alone, as it stood in 1772, compared with the whole trade of England to all parts of the world (the Colonies included) in the year 1704. They are from good vouchers; the latter period from the accounts on your table, the earlier from an original manuscript of Davenant, who first established the Inspector-General's office, which has been ever since his time so abundant a source of Parliamentary information.

The export trade to the Colonies consists of three great branches: the African — which, terminating almost wholly in the Colonies, must be put to the account of their commerce, — the West Indian, and the North American. All these are so interwoven that the attempt to separate them would tear to pieces the contexture of the whole; and, if not entirely destroy, would very much depreciate the value of all the parts. I therefore consider these three denominations to be, what in effect they are, one trade.

The trade to the Colonies, taken on the export side, at the beginning of this century, that is, in the year 1704, stood thus: —

Exports to North America and the West Indies . £483,265
To Africa 86,665
_____
£569,930

In the year 1772, which I take as a middle year between the highest and lowest of those lately laid on your table, the account was as follows: —

To North America and the West Indies . .	£4,791,734
To Africa	866,398
To which, if you add the export trade from Scotland, which had in 1704 no existence . .	364,000
	£6,022,132

From five hundred and odd thousand, it has grown to six millions. It has increased no less than twelve-fold. This is the state of the Colony trade as compared with itself at these two periods within this century; — and this is matter for meditation. But this is not all. Examine my second account. See how the export trade to the Colonies alone in 1772 stood in the other point of view; that is, as compared to the whole trade of England in 1704 : —

The whole export trade of England, including that to the Colonies, in 1704	£6,509,000
Export to the Colonies alone, in 1772 . . .	6,024,000
Difference,	£485,000

The trade with America alone is now within less than £500,000 of being equal to what this great commercial nation, England, carried on at the beginning of this century with the whole world! If I had taken the largest year of those on your table, it would rather have exceeded. But, it will be said, is not this American trade an unnatural protuberance, that has drawn the juices from the rest of the body? The reverse. It is the very food that has nourished every other part into its present magnitude. Our general trade has been greatly augmented, and augmented more or less in almost every part to which it ever extended; but with this material difference, that of the six millions which in the beginning of the century constituted the whole mass of our export commerce, the Colony trade was but one-twelfth part; it is now (as a part of sixteen millions) considerably more than a third of the whole. This is the relative proportion of the importance of the Colonies at these two periods; and all reasoning concerning our mode of treating them must have this proportion as its basis; or it is a reasoning weak, rotten, and sophistical.

Mr. Speaker, I cannot prevail on myself to hurry over this great consideration. *It is good for us to be here.* We stand where we have an immense view of what is, and what is past. Clouds, indeed, and darkness, rest upon the future. Let us, however, before we descend from this noble eminence, reflect that this growth of our national prosperity has happened within the short period of the life of man. It has happened within sixty-eight years. There are those alive whose memory might touch the two extremities. For instance, my Lord Bathurst might remember all the stages of the progress. He was in 1704 of an age at least to be made to comprehend such things. He was then old enough *acta parentum jam legere, et quae sit potuit cognoscere virtus.* Suppose, Sir, that the angel of this auspicious youth, foreseeing the many virtues which made him one of the most amiable, as he is one of the most fortunate, men of his age, had opened to him in vision that when in the fourth generation the third Prince of the House of Brunswick had sat twelve years on the throne of that nation which, by the happy issue of moderate and healing counsels, was to be made Great Britain, he should see his son, Lord Chancellor of England, turn back the current of hereditary dignity to its fountain, and raise him to a higher rank of peerage, whilst he enriched the family with a new one — if, amidst these bright and happy scenes of domestic honor and prosperity, that angel should have drawn up the curtain, and unfolded the rising glories of his country, and, whilst he was gazing with admiration on the then commercial grandeur of England, the genius should point out to him a little speck, scarcely visible in the mass of the national interest, a small seminal principle, rather than a formed body, and should tell him: " Young man, there is America — which at this day serves for little more than to amuse you with stories of savage men, and uncouth manners; yet shall, before you taste of death, show itself equal to the whole of that commerce which now attracts the envy of the world. Whatever England has been growing to by a progressive increase of improvement, brought in by varieties of people, by succession of civilizing conquests and civilizing settlements in a series of seventeen hundred years, you shall see as much added to her by America in the course of a single life!" If this state of his country had been foretold to him, would it not require all the sanguine credulity of youth, and all the fervid glow of enthusiasm, to make him believe it? Fortunate man, he has lived to see it! Fortunate, indeed, if he lives to see nothing that shall vary the prospect, and cloud the setting of his day!

Excuse me, Sir, if turning from such thoughts I resume this comparative view once more. You have seen it on a large scale; look at it on a small one. I will point out to your attention a particular instance of it in the single province of Pennsylvania. In the year 1704 that province called for £11,459 in value of your commodities, native and foreign. This was the whole. What did it demand in 1772? Why, nearly fifty times as much; for in that year the export to Pennsylvania was £507,909, nearly equal to the export to all the Colonies together in the first period.

I choose, Sir, to enter into these minute and particular details, because generalities, which in all other cases are apt to heighten and raise the subject, have here a tendency to sink it. When we speak of the commerce with our Colonies, fiction lags after truth, invention is unfruitful, and imagination cold and barren.

So far, Sir, as to the importance of the object, in view of its commerce, as concerned in the exports from England. If I were to detail the imports, I could show how many enjoyments they procure which deceive the burthen of life; how many materials which invigorate the springs of national industry, and extend and animate every part of our foreign and domestic commerce. This would be a curious subject indeed; but I must prescribe bounds to myself in a matter so vast and various.

I pass, therefore, to the Colonies in another point of view, their agriculture. This they have prosecuted with such a spirit, that, besides feeding plentifully their own growing multitude, their annual export of grain, comprehending rice, has some years ago exceeded a million in value. Of their last harvest I am persuaded they will export much more. At the beginning of the century some of these Colonies imported corn from the Mother Country. For some time past the Old World has been fed from the New. The scarcity which you have felt would have been a desolating famine, if this child of your old age, with a true filial piety, with a Roman charity, had not put the full breast of its youthful exuberance to the mouth of its exhausted parent.

As to the wealth which the Colonies have drawn from the sea by their fisheries, you had all that matter fully opened at your bar. You surely thought those acquisitions of value, for they seemed even to excite your envy; and yet the spirit by which that enterprising employment has been exercised ought rather, in my opinion, to have raised your esteem and admiration. And pray, Sir, what in the world is equal to it? Pass by the other parts, and look at the manner in which the people of New England have of late carried on the whale fishery. Whilst we follow them among the tumbling mountains of ice, and behold them penetrating into the deepest frozen recesses of Hudson's Bay and Davis's Straits, whilst we are looking for them beneath the arctic circle, we hear that they have pierced into the opposite region of polar cold, that they are at the antipodes, and engaged under the frozen Serpent of the south. Falkland Island, which seemed too remote and romantic an object for the grasp of national ambition, is but a stage and resting-place in the progress of their victorious industry. Nor is the equinoctial heat more discouraging to them than the accumulated winter of both the poles. We know that whilst some of them draw the line and strike the harpoon on the coast of Africa, others run the longitude and pursue their gigantic game along the coast of Brazil. No sea but what is vexed by their fisheries; no climate that is not witness to their toils. Neither the perseverance of Holland, nor the activity of France, nor the dexterous and firm sagacity of English enterprise ever carried this most perilous mode of hardy industry to the extent to which it has been pushed by this recent people; a people who are still, as it were, but in the gristle, and not yet hardened into the bone of manhood. When I contemplate these things; when I know that the Colonies in general owe little or nothing to any care of ours, and that they are not squeezed into this happy form by the constraints of watchful and suspicious government, but that, through a wise and salutary neglect, a generous nature has been suffered to take her own way to perfection; when I reflect upon these effects, when I see how profitable they have been to us, I feel all the pride of power sink, and all presumption in the wisdom of human contrivances melt and die away within me. My rigor relents. I pardon something to the spirit of liberty.

I am sensible, Sir, that all which I have asserted in my
5 detail is admitted in the gross: but that quite a different conclusion is drawn from it. America, gentlemen say, is a noble object. It is an object well worth fighting for. Certainly it is, if fighting a people be the best way of gaining them. Gentlemen in this respect will be led
10 to their choice of means by their complexions and their habits. Those who understand the military art will of course have some predilection for it. Those who wield the thunder of the state may have more confidence in the efficacy of arms. But I confess, possibly for want of this
15 knowledge, my opinion is much more in favor of prudent management than of force; considering force not as an odious, but a feeble instrument for preserving a people so numerous, so active, so growing, so spirited as this, in a profitable and subordinate connection with us.
20 First. Sir, permit me to observe that the use of force alone is but temporary. It may subdue for a moment, but it does not remove the necessity of subduing again; and a nation is not governed which is perpetually to be conquered.
25 My next objection is its uncertainty. Terror is not always the effect of force, and an armament is not a victory. If you do not succeed, you are without resource; for, conciliation failing, force remains; but, force failing, no further hope of reconciliation is left. Power and
30 authority are sometimes bought by kindness; but they can never be begged as alms by an impoverished and defeated violence.

A further objection to force is, that you impair the object by your very endeavors to preserve it. The thing
35 you fought for is not the thing which you recover; but

depreciated, sunk, wasted, and consumed in the contest. Nothing less will content me than *whole America*. I do not choose to consume its strength along with our own, because in all parts it is the British strength that I consume. I do not choose to be caught by a foreign enemy at the end of this exhausting conflict; and still less in the midst of it. I may escape; but I can make no insurance against such an event. Let me add, that I do not choose wholly to break the American spirit; because it is the spirit that has made the country.

Lastly, we have no sort of experience in favor of force as an instrument in the rule of our Colonies. Their growth and their utility has been owing to methods altogether different. Our ancient indulgence has been said to be pursued to a fault. It may be so. But we know, if feeling is evidence, that our fault was more tolerable than our attempt to mend it; and our sin far more salutary than our penitence.

These, Sir, are my reasons for not entertaining that high opinion of untried force by which many gentlemen, for whose sentiments in other particulars I have great respect, seem to be so greatly captivated. But there is still behind a third consideration concerning this object which serves to determine my opinion on the sort of policy which ought to be pursued in the management of America, even more than its population and its commerce — I mean its temper and character.

In this character of the Americans, a love of freedom is the predominating feature which marks and distinguishes the whole; and as an ardent is always a jealous affection, your Colonies become suspicious, restive, and untractable whenever they see the least attempt to wrest from them by force, or shuffle from them by chicane, what they think the only advantage worth living for. This fierce spirit of liberty is stronger in the English

Colonies probably than in any other people of the earth, and this from a great variety of powerful causes; which, to understand the true temper of their minds and the direction which this spirit takes, it will not be amiss to
5 lay open somewhat more largely.

First, the people of the Colonies are descendants of Englishmen. England, Sir, is a nation which still, I hope, respects, and formerly adored, her freedom. The Colonists emigrated from you when this part of your
10 character was most predominant; and they took this bias and direction the moment they parted from your hands. They are therefore not only devoted to liberty, but to liberty according to English ideas, and on English principles. Abstract liberty, like other mere abstrac-
15 tions, is not to be found. Liberty inheres in some sensible object; and every nation has formed to itself some favorite point, which by way of eminence becomes the criterion of their happiness. It happened, you know, Sir, that the great contests for freedom in this country
20 were from the earliest times chiefly upon the question of taxing. Most of the contests in the ancient commonwealths turned primarily on the right of election of magistrates; or on the balance among the several orders of the state. The question of money was not with them
25 so immediate. But in England it was otherwise. On this point of taxes the ablest pens, and most eloquent tongues, have been exercised; the greatest spirits have acted and suffered. In order to give the fullest satisfaction concerning the importance of this point, it was not
30 only necessary for those who in argument defended the excellence of the English Constitution to insist on this privilege of granting money as a dry point of fact, and to prove that the right had been acknowledged in ancient parchments and blind usages to reside in a certain body
35 called a House of Commons. They went much farther;

they attempted to prove, and they succeeded, that in theory it ought to be so, from the particular nature of a House of Commons as an immediate representative of the people, whether the old records had delivered this oracle or not. They took infinite pains to inculcate, as a fundamental principle, that in all monarchies the people must in effect themselves, mediately or immediately, possess the power of granting their own money, or no shadow of liberty can subsist. The Colonies draw from you, as with their life-blood, these ideas and principles. Their love of liberty, as with you, fixed and attached on this specific point of taxing. Liberty might be safe, or might be endangered, in twenty other particulars, without their being much pleased or alarmed. Here they felt its pulse; and as they found that beat, they thought themselves sick or sound. I do not say whether they were right or wrong in applying your general arguments to their own case. It is not easy, indeed, to make a monopoly of theorems and corollaries. The fact is, that they did thus apply those general arguments; and your mode of governing them, whether through lenity or indolence, through wisdom or mistake, confirmed them in the imagination that they, as well as you, had an interest in these common principles.

They were further confirmed in this pleasing error by the form of their provincial legislative assemblies. Their governments are popular in an high degree; some are merely popular; in all, the popular representative is the most weighty; and this share of the people in their ordinary government never fails to inspire them with lofty sentiments, and with a strong aversion from whatever tends to deprive them of their chief importance.

If anything were wanting to this necessary operation of the form of government, religion would have given it a complete effect. Religion, always a principle of energy,

in this new people is no way worn out or impaired; and
their mode of professing it is also one main cause of this
free spirit. The people are Protestants; and of that
kind which is the most adverse to all implicit submission
of mind and opinion. This is a persuasion not only
favorable to liberty, but built upon it. I do not think,
Sir, that the reason of this averseness in the dissenting
churches from all that looks like absolute government is
so much to be sought in their religious tenets, as in their
history. Every one knows that the Roman Catholic
religion is at least co-eval with most of the governments
where it prevails; that it has generally gone hand in
hand with them, and received great favor and every kind
of support from authority. The Church of England too
was formed from her cradle under the nursing care of
regular government. But the dissenting interests have
sprung up in direct opposition to all the ordinary powers
of the world, and could justify that opposition only on
a strong claim to natural liberty. Their very existence
depended on the powerful and unremitted assertion of
that claim. All Protestantism, even the most cold and
passive, is a sort of dissent. But the religion most
prevalent in our Northern Colonies is a refinement on
the principle of resistance; it is the dissidence of dissent, and the protestantism of the Protestant religion.
This religion, under a variety of denominations agreeing
in nothing but in the communion of the spirit of liberty,
is predominant in most of the Northern Provinces, where
the Church of England, notwithstanding its legal rights,
is in reality no more than a sort of private sect, not com-
posing most probably the tenth of the people. The
Colonists left England when this spirit was high, and in
the emigrants was the highest of all; and even that
stream of foreigners which has been constantly flowing
into these Colonies has, for the greatest part, been com-

posed of dissenters from the establishments of their several countries, who have brought with them a temper and character far from alien to that of the people with whom they mixed.

Sir, I can perceive by their manner that some gentlemen object to the latitude of this description, because in the Southern Colonies the Church of England forms a large body, and has a regular establishment. It is certainly true. There is, however, a circumstance attending these Colonies which, in my opinion, fully counterbalances this difference, and makes the spirit of liberty still more high and haughty than in those to the northward. It is that in Virginia and the Carolinas they have a vast multitude of slaves. Where this is the case in any part of the world, those who are free are by far the most proud and jealous of their freedom. Freedom is to them not only an enjoyment, but a kind of rank and privilege. Not seeing there, that freedom, as in countries where it is a common blessing and as broad and general as the air, may be united with much abject toil, with great misery, with all the exterior of servitude; liberty looks, amongst them, like something that is more noble and liberal. I do not mean, Sir, to commend the superior morality of this sentiment, which has at least as much pride as virtue in it; but I cannot alter the nature of man. The fact is so; and these people of the Southern Colonies are much more strongly, and with an higher and more stubborn spirit, attached to liberty than those to the northward. Such were all the ancient commonwealths; such were our Gothic ancestors; such in our days were the Poles; and such will be all masters of slaves, who are not slaves themselves. In such a people the haughtiness of domination combines with the spirit of freedom, fortifies it, and renders it invincible.

Permit me, Sir, to add another circumstance in our

Colonies which contributes no mean part towards the growth and effect of this untractable spirit. I mean their education. In no country perhaps in the world is the law so general a study. The profession itself is numerous and powerful; and in most provinces it takes the lead. The greater number of the deputies sent to the Congress were lawyers. But all who read, and most do read, endeavor to obtain some smattering in that science. I have been told by an eminent bookseller, that in no branch of his business, after tracts of popular devotion, were so many books as those on the law exported to the Plantations. The Colonists have now fallen into the way of printing them for their own use. I hear that they have sold nearly as many of Blackstone's Commentaries in America as in England. General Gage marks out this disposition very particularly in a letter on your table. He states that all the people in his government are lawyers, or smatterers in law; and that in Boston they have been enabled, by successful chicane, wholly to evade many parts of one of your capital penal constitutions. The smartness of debate will say that this knowledge ought to teach them more clearly the rights of legislature, their obligations to obedience, and the penalties of rebellion. All this is mighty well. But my honorable and learned friend on the floor, who condescends to mark what I say for animadversion, will disdain that ground. He has heard, as well as I, that when great honors and great emoluments do not win over this knowledge to the service of the state, it is a formidable adversary to government. If the spirit be not tamed and broken by these happy methods, it is stubborn and litigious. *Abeunt studia in mores.* This study renders men acute, inquisitive, dexterous, prompt in attack, ready in defence, full of resources. In other countries, the people, more simple, and of a less mercurial cast, judge of an ill principle in government only by an actual grievance; here they anticipate the evil, and judge of the pressure of the grievance by the badness of the principle. They augur misgovernment at a distance, and snuff the approach of tyranny in every tainted breeze.

The last cause of this disobedient spirit in the Colonies is hardly less powerful than the rest, as it is not merely moral, but laid deep in the natural constitution of things. Three thousand miles of ocean lie between you and them. No contrivance can prevent the effect of this distance in weakening government. Seas roll, and months pass, between the order and the execution; and the want of a speedy explanation of a single point is enough to defeat a whole system. You have, indeed, winged ministers of vengeance, who carry your bolts in their pounces to the remotest verge of the sea. But there a power steps in that limits the arrogance of raging passions and furious elements, and says, *So far shalt thou go, and no farther.* Who are you, that you should fret and rage, and bite the chains of nature? Nothing worse happens to you than does to all nations who have extensive empire; and it happens in all the forms into which empire can be thrown. In large bodies the circulation of power must be less vigorous at the extremities. Nature has said it. The Turk cannot govern Egypt and Arabia and Kurdistan as he governs Thrace; nor has he the same dominion in Crimea and Algiers which he has at Brusa and Smyrna. Despotism itself is obliged to truck and huckster. The Sultan gets such obedience as he can. He governs with a loose rein, that he may govern at all; and the whole of the force and vigor of his authority in his centre is derived from a prudent relaxation in all his borders. Spain, in her provinces, is, perhaps, not so well obeyed as you are in yours. She complies, too; she submits; she watches times. This is the immutable condition, the eternal law of extensive and detached empire.

Then, Sir, from these six capital sources — of descent, of form of government, of religion in the Northern Provinces, of manners in the Southern, of education, of the remoteness of situation from the first mover of government — from all these causes a fierce spirit of liberty has grown up. It has grown with the growth of the people in your Colonies, and increased with the increase of their wealth; a spirit that unhappily meeting with an exercise of power in England which, however lawful, is not reconcilable to any ideas of liberty, much less with theirs, has kindled this flame that is ready to consume us.

I do not mean to commend either the spirit in this excess, or the moral causes which produce it. Perhaps a more smooth and accommodating spirit of freedom in them would be more acceptable to us. Perhaps ideas of liberty might be desired more reconcilable with an arbitrary and boundless authority. Perhaps we might wish the Colonists to be persuaded that their liberty is more secure when held in trust for them by us, as their guardians during a perpetual minority, than with any part of it in their own hands. The question is, not whether their spirit deserves praise or blame, but — what, in the name of God, shall we do with it? You have before you the object, such as it is, with all its glories, with all its imperfections on its head. You see the magnitude, the importance, the temper, the habits, the disorders. By all these considerations we are strongly urged to determine something concerning it. We are called upon to fix some rule and line for our future conduct which may give a little stability to our politics, and prevent the return of such unhappy deliberations as the present. Every such return will bring the matter before us in a still more untractable form. For, what astonishing and incredible things have we not seen already! What monsters have not been generated from this unnatural contention! Whilst every principle of authority and resistance has been pushed, upon both sides, as far as it would go, there is nothing so solid and certain, either in reasoning or in practice, that has not been shaken. Until very lately all authority in America seemed to be nothing but an emanation from yours. Even the popular part of the Colony Constitution derived all its activity and its first vital movement from the pleasure of the Crown. We thought, Sir, that the utmost which the discontented Colonists could do was to disturb authority; we never dreamt they could of themselves supply it — knowing in general what an operose business it is to establish a government absolutely new. But having, for our purposes in this contention, resolved that none but an obedient Assembly should sit, the humors of the people there, finding all passage through the legal channel stopped, with great violence broke out another way. Some provinces have tried their experiment, as we have tried ours; and theirs has succeeded. They have formed a government sufficient for its purposes, without the bustle of a revolution or the troublesome formality of an election. Evident necessity and tacit consent have done the business in an instant. So well they have done it, that Lord Dunmore — the account is among the fragments on your table — tells you that the new institution is infinitely better obeyed than the ancient government ever was in its most fortunate periods. Obedience is what makes government, and not the names by which it is called; not the name of Governor, as formerly, or Committee, as at present. This new government has originated directly from the people, and was not transmitted through any of the ordinary artificial media of a positive constitution. It was not a manufacture ready formed, and transmitted to them in that condition from England. The evil arising from hence is this; that the Colonists having once found the possibility of enjoying the advantages of order in the midst of a struggle for liberty, such struggles will not henceforward seem so terrible to the settled and sober part of mankind as they had appeared before the trial.

Pursuing the same plan of punishing by the denial of the exercise of government to still greater lengths, we wholly abrogated the ancient government of Massachusetts. We were confident that the first feeling, if not the very prospect, of anarchy would instantly enforce a complete submission. The experiment was tried. A new, strange, unexpected face of things appeared. Anarchy is found tolerable. A vast province has now subsisted, and subsisted in a considerable degree of health and vigor for near a twelvemonth, without Governor, without public Council, without judges, without executive magistrates. How long it will continue in this state, or what may arise out of this unheard-of situation, how can the wisest of us conjecture? Our late experience has taught us that many of those fundamental principles, formerly believed infallible, are either not of the importance they were imagined to be, or that we have not at all adverted to some other far more important and far more powerful principles, which entirely overrule those we had considered as omnipotent. I am much against any further experiments which tend to put to the proof any more of these allowed opinions which contribute so much to the public tranquillity. In effect, we suffer as much at home by this loosening of all ties, and this concussion of all established opinions, as we do abroad; for in order to prove that the Americans have no right to their liberties, we are every day endeavoring to subvert the maxims which preserve the whole spirit of our own.

To prove that the Americans ought not to be free, we are obliged to depreciate the value of freedom itself; and we never seem to gain a paltry advantage over them in debate without attacking some of those principles, or deriding some of those feelings, for which our ancestors have shed their blood.

But, Sir, in wishing to put an end to pernicious experiments, I do not mean to preclude the fullest inquiry. Far from it. Far from deciding on a sudden or partial view, I would patiently go round and round the subject, and survey it minutely in every possible aspect. Sir, if I were capable of engaging you to an equal attention, I would state that, as far as I am capable of discerning, there are but three ways of proceeding relative to this stubborn spirit which prevails in your Colonies, and disturbs your government. These are — to change that spirit, as inconvenient, by removing the causes; to prosecute it as criminal; or to comply with it as necessary. I would not be guilty of an imperfect enumeration; I can think of but these three. Another has indeed been started, — that of giving up the Colonies; but it met so slight a reception that I do not think myself obliged to dwell a great while upon it. It is nothing but a little sally of anger, like the frowardness of peevish children, who, when they cannot get all they would have, are resolved to take nothing.

The first of these plans — to change the spirit, as inconvenient, by removing the causes — I think is the most like a systematic proceeding. It is radical in its principle; but it is attended with great difficulties, some of them little short, as I conceive, of impossibilities. This will appear by examining into the plans which have been proposed.

As the growing population in the Colonies is evidently one cause of their resistance, it was last session mentioned in both Houses, by men of weight, and received not without applause, that in order to check this evil it would be proper for the Crown to make no further grants of land. But to this scheme there are two objections. The first, that there is already so much unsettled land in private hands as to afford room for an immense future population, although the Crown not only withheld its grants, but annihilated its soil. If this be the case, then the only effect of this avarice of desolation, this hoarding of a royal wilderness, would be to raise the value of the possessions in the hands of the great private monopolists, without any adequate check to the growing and alarming mischief of population.

But if you stopped your grants, what would be the consequence? The people would occupy without grants. They have already so occupied in many places. You cannot station garrisons in every part of these deserts. If you drive the people from one place, they will carry on their annual tillage, and remove with their flocks and herds to another. Many of the people in the back settlements are already little attached to particular situations. Already they have topped the Appalachian Mountains. From thence they behold before them an immense plain, one vast, rich, level meadow; a square of five hundred miles. Over this they would wander without a possibility of restraint; they would change their manners with the habits of their life; would soon forget a government by which they were disowned; would become hordes of English Tartars; and, pouring down upon your unfortified frontiers a fierce and irresistible cavalry, become masters of your governors and your counsellors, your collectors and comptrollers, and of all the slaves that adhered to them. Such would, and in no long time must be, the effect of attempting to forbid as a crime and to suppress as an evil the command and blessing of providence, *Increase and multiply.* Such would be the happy result of the endeavor to keep as a lair of wild beasts that earth which God, by an express charter, has given to the children of men. Far different, and surely much wiser, has been our policy hitherto. Hitherto we have invited our people, by every kind of bounty, to fixed establishments. We have invited the husbandman to look to authority for his title. We have taught him piously to believe in the mysterious virtue of wax and parchment. We have thrown each tract of land, as it was peopled, into districts, that the ruling power should never be wholly out of sight. We have settled all we could; and we have carefully attended every settlement with government.

Adhering, Sir, as I do, to this policy, as well as for the reasons I have just given, I think this new project of hedging-in population to be neither prudent nor practicable.

To impoverish the Colonies in general, and in particular to arrest the noble course of their marine enterprises, would be a more easy task. I freely confess it. We have shown a disposition to a system of this kind, a disposition even to continue the restraint after the offence, looking on ourselves as rivals to our Colonies, and persuaded that of course we must gain all that they shall lose. Much mischief we may certainly do. The power inadequate to all other things is often more than sufficient for this. I do not look on the direct and immediate power of the Colonies to resist our violence as very formidable. In this, however, I may be mistaken. But when I consider that we have Colonies for no purpose but to be serviceable to us, it seems to my poor understanding a little preposterous to make them unserviceable in order to keep them obedient. It is, in truth, nothing more than the old and, as I thought, exploded problem of tyranny, which proposes to beggar its subjects into submission. But remember, when you have completed your system of impoverishment, that nature still proceeds in her ordinary course; that discontent will increase with misery; and that there are critical moments in the fortune of all states when they who are too weak to contribute to your prosperity may be strong enough to complete your ruin. *Spoliatis arma supersunt.*

The temper and character which prevail in our Colonies are, I am afraid, unalterable by any human art. We cannot, I fear, falsify the pedigree of this fierce people, and persuade them that they are not sprung from a nation in whose veins the blood of freedom circulates. The language in which they would hear you tell them this tale would detect the imposition; your speech would betray you. An Englishman is the unfittest person on earth to argue another Englishman into slavery.

I think it is nearly as little in our power to change their republican religion as their free descent: or to substitute the Roman Catholic as a penalty, or the Church of England as an improvement. The mode of inquisition and dragooning is going out of fashion in the Old World, and I should not confide much to their efficacy in the New. The education of the Americans is also on the same unalterable bottom with their religion. You cannot persuade them to burn their books of curious science; to banish their lawyers from their courts of laws; or to quench the lights of their assemblies by refusing to choose those persons who are best read in their privileges. It would be no less impracticable to think of wholly annihilating the popular assemblies in which these lawyers sit. The army, by which we must govern in their place, would be far more chargeable to us, not quite so effectual, and perhaps in the end full as difficult to be kept in obedience.

With regard to the high aristocratic spirit of Virginia and the Southern Colonies, it has been proposed, I know, to reduce it by declaring a general enfranchisement of their slaves. This object has had its advocates and panegyrists; yet I never could argue myself into any opinion of it. Slaves are often much attached to their masters. A general wild offer of liberty would not always be accepted. History furnishes few instances of it. It is sometimes as hard to persuade slaves to be free, as it is to compel freemen to be slaves; and in this auspicious scheme we should have both these pleasing tasks on our hands at once. But when we talk of enfranchisement, do we not perceive that the American master may enfranchise too, and arm servile hands in defence of freedom? — a measure to which other people have had recourse more than once, and not without success, in a desperate situation of their affairs.

Slaves as these unfortunate black people are, and dull as all men are from slavery, must they not a little suspect the offer of freedom from that very nation which has sold them to their present masters? — from that nation, one of whose causes of quarrel with those masters is their refusal to deal any more in that inhuman traffic? An offer of freedom from England would come rather oddly, shipped to them in an African vessel which is refused an entry into the ports of Virginia or Carolina with a cargo of three hundred Angola negroes. It would be curious to see the Guinea captain attempting at the same instant to publish his proclamation of liberty, and to advertise his sale of slaves.

But let us suppose all these moral difficulties got over. The ocean remains. You cannot pump this dry; and as long as it continues in its present bed, so long all the causes which weaken authority by distance will continue.

> "Ye gods, annihilate but space and time,
> And make two lovers happy!"

was a pious and passionate prayer; but just as reasonable as many of the serious wishes of grave and solemn politicians.

If then, Sir, it seems almost desperate to think of any alternative course for changing the moral causes, and not quite easy to remove the natural, which produce prejudices irreconcilable to the late exercise of our authority — but that the spirit infallibly will continue, and, continuing, will produce such effects as now embarrass us — the second mode under consideration is to prosecute that spirit in its overt acts as criminal.

At this proposition I must pause a moment. The thing seems a great deal too big for my ideas of jurisprudence. It should seem to my way of conceiving such matters that there is a very wide difference, in reason and policy, between the mode of proceeding on the irregular conduct of scattered individuals, or even of bands of men who disturb order within the state, and the civil dissensions which may, from time to time, on great questions, agitate the several communities which compose a great empire. It looks to me to be narrow and pedantic to apply the ordinary ideas of criminal justice to this great public contest. I do not know the method of drawing up an indictment against a whole people. I cannot insult and ridicule the feelings of millions of my fellow-creatures as Sir Edward Coke insulted one excellent individual (Sir Walter Raleigh) at the bar. I hope I am not ripe to pass sentence on the gravest public bodies, intrusted with magistracies of great authority and dignity, and charged with the safety of their fellow-citizens, upon the very same title that I am. I really think that, for wise men, this is not judicious; for sober men, not decent; for minds tinctured with humanity, not mild and merciful.

Perhaps, Sir, I am mistaken in my idea of an empire,

as distinguished from a single state or kingdom. But my idea of it is this, that an empire is the aggregate of many states under one common head, whether this head be a monarch or a presiding republic. It does, in such constitutions, frequently happen — and nothing but the dismal, cold, dead uniformity of servitude can prevent its happening — that the subordinate parts have many local privileges and immunities. Between these privileges and the supreme common authority the line may be extremely nice. Of course disputes, often, too, very bitter disputes, and much ill blood, will arise. But though every privilege is an exemption, in the case, from the ordinary exercise of the supreme authority, it is no denial of it. The claim of a privilege seems rather, *ex vi termini*, to imply a superior power; for to talk of the privileges of a state or of a person who has no superior is hardly any better than speaking nonsense. Now, in such unfortunate quarrels among the component parts of a great political union of communities, I can scarcely conceive anything more completely imprudent than for the head of the empire to insist that, if any privilege is pleaded against his will or his acts, his whole authority is denied; instantly to proclaim rebellion, to beat to arms, and to put the offending provinces under the ban. Will not this, Sir, very soon teach the provinces to make no distinctions on their part? Will it not teach them that the government, against which a claim of liberty is tantamount to high treason, is a government to which submission is equivalent to slavery? It may not always be quite convenient to impress dependent communities with such an idea.

We are, indeed, in all disputes with the Colonies, by the necessity of things, the judge. It is true, Sir. But I confess that the character of judge in my own cause is a thing that frightens me. Instead of filling me with pride. I am exceedingly humbled by it. I cannot proceed with a stern, assured, judicial confidence, until I find myself in something more like a judicial character. I must have these hesitations as long as I am compelled to recollect that, in my little reading upon such contests as these, the sense of mankind has at least as often decided against the superior as the subordinate power. Sir, let me add, too, that the opinion of my having some abstract right in my favor would not put me much at my ease in passing sentence, unless I could be sure that there were no rights which, in their exercise under certain circumstances, were not the most odious of all wrongs and the most vexatious of all injustice. Sir, these considerations have great weight with me when I find things so circumstanced, that I see the same party at once a civil litigant against me in point of right and a culprit before me, while I sit as a criminal judge on acts of his whose moral quality is to be decided upon the merits of that very litigation. Men are every now and then put, by the complexity of human affairs, into strange situations; but justice is the same, let the judge be in what situation he will.

There is, Sir, also a circumstance which convinces me that this mode of criminal proceeding is not, at least in the present stage of our contest, altogether expedient; which is nothing less than the conduct of those very persons who have seemed to adopt that mode by lately declaring a rebellion in Massachusetts Bay, as they had formerly addressed to have traitors brought hither, under an Act of Henry the Eighth, for trial. For though rebellion is declared, it is not proceeded against as such, nor have any steps been taken towards the apprehension or conviction of any individual offender, either on our late or our former Address; but modes of public coercion have been adopted, and such as have much more resemblance to a sort of qualified hostility towards an independent power than the punishment of rebellious subjects. All this seems rather inconsistent; but it shows how difficult it is to apply these juridical ideas to our present case.

In this situation, let us seriously and coolly ponder. What is it we have got by all our menaces, which have been many and ferocious? What advantage have we derived from the penal laws we have passed, and which, for the time, have been severe and numerous? What advances have we made towards our object by the sending of a force which, by land and sea, is no contemptible strength? Has the disorder abated? Nothing less. When I see things in this situation after such confident hopes, bold promises, and active exertions, I cannot, for my life, avoid a suspicion that the plan itself is not correctly right.

If, then, the removal of the causes of this spirit of American liberty be for the greater part, or rather entirely, impracticable; if the ideas of criminal process be inapplicable — or, if applicable, are in the highest degree inexpedient; what way yet remains? No way is open but the third and last, — to comply with the American spirit as necessary; or, if you please, to submit to it as a necessary evil.

If we adopt this mode, — if we mean to conciliate and concede, — let us see of what nature the concession ought to be. To ascertain the nature of our concession, we must look at their complaint. The Colonies complain that they have not the characteristic mark and seal of British freedom. They complain that they are taxed in a Parliament in which they are not represented. If you mean to satisfy them at all, you must satisfy them with regard to this complaint. If you mean to please any people you must give them the boon which they ask;

not what you may think better for them, but of a kind totally different. Such an act may be a wise regulation, but it is no concession; whereas our present theme is the mode of giving satisfaction.

5 Sir, I think you must perceive that I am resolved this day to have nothing at all to do with the question of the right of taxation. Some gentlemen startle — but it is true; I put it totally out of the question. It is less than nothing in my consideration. I do not indeed won-
10 der, nor will you, Sir, that gentlemen of profound learning are fond of displaying it on this profound subject. But my consideration is narrow, confined, and wholly limited to the policy of the question. I do not examine whether the giving away a man's money be a power ex-
15 cepted and reserved out of the general trust of government, and how far all mankind, in all forms of polity, are entitled to an exercise of that right by the charter of nature; or whether, on the contrary, a right of taxation is necessarily involved in the general principle of
20 legislation, and inseparable from the ordinary supreme power. These are deep questions, where great names militate against each other, where reason is perplexed, and an appeal to authorities only thickens the confusion; for high and reverend authorities lift up their
25 heads on both sides, and there is no sure footing in the middle. This point is the great

"Serbonian bog,
Betwixt Damiata and Mount Casius old,
Where armies whole have sunk."

30 I do not intend to be overwhelmed in that bog, though in such respectable company. The question with me is, not whether you have a right to render your people miserable, but whether it is not your interest to make them happy. It is not what a lawyer tells me I *may* do, but
35 what humanity, reason, and justice tell me I *ought* to

do. Is a politic act the worse for being a generous one? Is no concession proper but that which is made from your want of right to keep what you grant? Or does it lessen the grace or dignity of relaxing in the exercise of an odious claim because you have your evidence-room full of titles, and your magazines stuffed with arms to enforce them? What signify all those titles, and all those arms? Of what avail are they, when the reason of the thing tells me that the assertion of my title is the loss of my suit, and that I could do nothing but wound myself by the use of my own weapons?

Such is steadfastly my opinion of the absolute necessity of keeping up the concord of this Empire by an unity of spirit, though in a diversity of operations, that, if I were sure the Colonists had, at their leaving this country, sealed a regular compact of servitude; that they had solemnly abjured all the rights of citizens; that they had made a vow to renounce all ideas of liberty for them and their posterity to all generations; yet I should hold myself obliged to conform to the temper I found universally prevalent in my own day, and to govern two million of men, impatient of servitude, on the principles of freedom. I am not determining a point of law, I am restoring tranquillity; and the general character and situation of a people must determine what sort of government is fitted for them. That point nothing else can or ought to determine.

My idea, therefore, without considering whether we yield as matter of right, or grant as matter of favor, is to admit the people of our Colonies into an interest in the Constitution; and, by recording that admission in the journals of Parliament, to give them as strong an assurance as the nature of the thing will admit, that we mean forever to adhere to that solemn declaration of systematic indulgence.

Some years ago the repeal of a revenue Act, upon its understood principle, might have served to show that we intended an unconditional abatement of the exercise of a taxing power. Such a measure was then sufficient to remove all suspicion, and to give perfect content. But unfortunate events since that time may make something further necessary; and not more necessary for the satisfaction of the Colonies than for the dignity and consistency of our own future proceedings.

I have taken a very incorrect measure of the disposition of the House if this proposal in itself would be received with dislike. I think, Sir, we have few American financiers. But our misfortune is, we are too acute, we are too exquisite in our conjectures of the future, for men oppressed with such great and present evils. The more moderate among the opposers of Parliamentary concession freely confess that they hope no good from taxation, but they apprehend the Colonists have further views: and if this point were conceded, they would instantly attack the trade laws. These gentlemen are convinced that this was the intention from the beginning, and the quarrel of the Americans with taxation was no more than a cloak and cover to this design. Such has been the language even of a gentleman of real moderation, and of a natural temper well adjusted to fair and equal government. I am, however, Sir, not a little surprised at this kind of discourse, whenever I hear it; and I am the more surprised on account of the arguments which I constantly find in company with it, and which are often urged from the same mouths and on the same day.

For instance, when we allege that it is against reason to tax a people under so many restraints in trade as the Americans, the noble lord in the blue ribbon shall tell you that the restraints on trade are futile and useless —

of no advantage to us, and of no burthen to those on
whom they are imposed; that the trade to America is
not secured by the Acts of Navigation, but by the natural and irresistible advantage of a commercial preference.

Such is the merit of the trade laws in this posture of
the debate. But when strong internal circumstances are
urged against the taxes; when the scheme is dissected;
when experience and the nature of things are brought to
prove, and do prove, the utter impossibility of obtaining
an effective revenue from the Colonies; when these
things are pressed, or rather press themselves, so as to
drive the advocates of Colony taxes to a clear admission
of the futility of the scheme; then, Sir, the sleeping
trade laws revive from their trance, and this useless taxation is to be kept sacred, not for its own sake, but as a
counter-guard and security of the laws of trade.

Then, Sir, you keep up revenue laws which are mischievous, in order to preserve trade laws that are useless.
Such is the wisdom of our plan in both its members.
They are separately given up as of no value, and yet one
is always to be defended for the sake of the other; but
I cannot agree with the noble lord, nor with the pamphlet from whence he seems to have borrowed these
ideas concerning the inutility of the trade laws. For,
without idolizing them, I am sure they are still, in many
ways, of great use to us; and in former times they have
been of the greatest. They do confine, and they do
greatly narrow, the market for the Americans; but my
perfect conviction of this does not help me in the least
to discern how the revenue laws form any security whatsoever to the commercial regulations, or that these commercial regulations are the true ground of the quarrel,
or that the giving way, in any one instance of authority,
is to lose all that may remain unconceded.

One fact is clear and indisputable. The public and

avowed origin of this quarrel was on taxation. This
quarrel has indeed brought on new disputes on new questions; but certainly the least bitter, and the fewest of
all, on the trade laws. To judge which of the two be
5 the real radical cause of quarrel, we have to see whether
the commercial dispute did, in order of time, precede the
dispute on taxation? There is not a shadow of evidence
for it. Next, to enable us to judge whether at this
moment a dislike to the trade laws be the real cause of
10 quarrel, it is absolutely necessary to put the taxes out
of the question by a repeal. See how the Americans act
in this position, and then you will be able to discern
correctly what is the true object of the controversy, or
whether any controversy at all will remain. Unless you
15 consent to remove this cause of difference, it is impossible, with decency, to assert that the dispute is not upon
what it is avowed to be. And I would, Sir, recommend
to your serious consideration whether it be prudent to
form a rule for punishing people, not on their own acts,
20 but on your conjectures? Surely it is preposterous at
the very best. It is not justifying your anger by their
misconduct, but it is converting your ill-will into their
delinquency.

But the Colonies will go further. Alas! alas! when
25 will this speculation against fact and reason end? What
will quiet these panic fears which we entertain of the
hostile effect of a conciliatory conduct? Is it true that
no case can exist in which it is proper for the sovereign
to accede to the desires of his discontented subjects?
30 Is there anything peculiar in this case to make a rule
for itself? Is all authority of course lost when it is not
pushed to the extreme? Is it a certain maxim that the
fewer causes of dissatisfaction are left by government,
the more the subject will be inclined to resist and rebel?
35   All these objections being in fact no more than sus-

picions, conjectures, divinations, formed in defiance of fact and experience, they did not, Sir, discourage me from entertaining the idea of a conciliatory concession founded on the principles which I have just stated.

In forming a plan for this purpose, I endeavored to put myself in that frame of mind which was the most natural and the most reasonable, and which was certainly the most probable means of securing me from all error. I set out with a perfect distrust of my own abilities, a total renunciation of every speculation of my own, and with a profound reverence for the wisdom of our ancestors who have left us the inheritance of so happy a constitution and so flourishing an empire, and, what is a thousand times more valuable, the treasury of the maxims and principles which formed the one and obtained the other.

During the reigns of the kings of Spain of the Austrian family, whenever they were at a loss in the Spanish councils, it was common for their statesmen to say that they ought to consult the genius of Philip the Second. The genius of Philip the Second might mislead them, and the issue of their affairs showed that they had not chosen the most perfect standard; but, Sir, I am sure that I shall not be misled when, in a case of constitutional difficulty, I consult the genius of the English Constitution. Consulting at that oracle — it was with all due humility and piety — I found four capital examples in a similar case before me; those of Ireland, Wales, Chester, and Durham.

Ireland, before the English conquest, though never governed by a despotic power, had no Parliament. How far the English Parliament itself was at that time modelled according to the present form is disputed among antiquaries; but we have all the reason in the world to be assured that a form of Parliament such as England

then enjoyed she instantly communicated to Ireland, and
we are equally sure that almost every successive improvement in constitutional liberty, as fast as it was made
here, was transmitted thither. The feudal baronage and
5 the feudal knighthood, the roots of our primitive Constitution, were early transplanted into that soil, and
grew and flourished there. Magna Charta, if it did not
give us originally the House of Commons, gave us at
least a House of Commons of weight and consequence.
10 But your ancestors did not churlishly sit down alone to
the feast of Magna Charta. Ireland was made immediately a partaker. This benefit of English laws and liberties, I confess, was not at first extended to all Ireland.
Mark the consequence. English authority and English
15 liberties had exactly the same boundaries. Your standard could never be advanced an inch before your privileges. Sir John Davis shows beyond a doubt that the
refusal of a general communication of these rights was
the true cause why Ireland was five hundred years in
20 subduing; and after the vain projects of a military government, attempted in the reign of Queen Elizabeth, it
was soon discovered that nothing could make that country English, in civility and allegiance, but your laws and
your forms of legislature. It was not English arms, but
25 the English Constitution, that conquered Ireland. From
that time Ireland has ever had a general Parliament, as
she had before a partial Parliament. You changed the
people; you altered the religion; but you never touched
the form or the vital substance of free government in
30 that Kingdom. You deposed kings; you restored them;
you altered the succession to theirs, as well as to your
own Crown; but you never altered their Constitution, the
principle of which was respected by usurpation, restored
with the restoration of monarchy, and established, I
35 trust, forever, by the glorious Revolution. This has

made Ireland the great and flourishing kingdom that it is, and, from a disgrace and a burthen intolerable to this nation, has rendered her a principal part of our strength and ornament. This country cannot be said to have ever formally taxed her. The irregular things done in the confusion of mighty troubles and on the hinge of great revolutions, even if all were done that is said to have been done, form no example. If they have any effect in argument, they make an exception to prove the rule. None of your own liberties could stand a moment, if the casual deviations from them at such times were suffered to be used as proofs of their nullity. By the lucrative amount of such casual breaches in the constitution, judge what the stated and fixed rule of supply has been in that kingdom. Your Irish pensioners would starve, if they had no other fund to live on than taxes granted by English authority. Turn your eyes to those popular grants from whence all your great supplies are come, and learn to respect that only source of public wealth in the British Empire.

My next example is Wales. This country was said to be reduced by Henry the Third. It was said more truly to be so by Edward the First. But though then conquered, it was not looked upon as any part of the realm of England. Its old Constitution, whatever that might have been, was destroyed, and no good one was substituted in its place. The care of that tract was put into the hands of Lords Marchers — a form of government of a very singular kind; a strange heterogeneous monster, something between hostility and government; perhaps it has a sort of resemblance, according to the modes of those terms, to that of Commander-in-chief at present, to whom all civil power is granted as secondary. The manners of the Welsh nation followed the genius of the government. The people were ferocious, restive, savage, and uncultivated; sometimes composed, never pacified. Wales, within itself, was in perpetual disorder, and it kept the frontier of England in perpetual alarm. Benefits from it to the state there were none. Wales was only known to England by incursion and invasion.

Sir, during that state of things, Parliament was not idle. They attempted to subdue the fierce spirit of the Welsh by all sorts of rigorous laws. They prohibited by statute the sending all sorts of arms into Wales, as you prohibit by proclamation (with something more of doubt on the legality) the sending arms to America. They disarmed the Welsh by statute, as you attempted (but still with more question on the legality) to disarm New England by an instruction. They made an Act to drag offenders from Wales into England for trial, as you have done (but with more hardship) with regard to America. By another Act, where one of the parties was an Englishman, they ordained that his trial should be always by English. They made Acts to restrain trade, as you do; and they prevented the Welsh from the use of fairs and markets, as you do the Americans from fisheries and foreign ports. In short, when the Statute Book was not quite so much swelled as it is now, you find no less than fifteen acts of penal regulation on the subject of Wales.

Here we rub our hands. — A fine body of precedents for the authority of Parliament and the use of it! — I admit it fully; and pray add likewise to these precedents that all the while Wales rid this Kingdom like an incubus, that it was an unprofitable and oppressive burthen, and that an Englishman travelling in that country could not go six yards from the high road without being murdered.

The march of the human mind is slow. Sir, it was not until after two hundred years discovered that, by an eternal law, providence had decreed vexation to violence, and poverty to rapine. Your ancestors did however at length open their eyes to the ill-husbandry of injustice. They found that the tyranny of a free people could of all tyrannies the least be endured, and that laws made against a whole nation were not the most effectual methods of securing its obedience. Accordingly, in the twenty-seventh year of Henry the Eighth the course was entirely altered. With a preamble stating the entire and perfect rights of the Crown of England, it gave to the Welsh all the rights and privileges of English subjects. A political order was established; the military power gave way to the civil; the Marches were turned into Counties. But that a nation should have a right to English liberties, and yet no share at all in the fundamental security of these liberties — the grant of their own property — seemed a thing so incongruous, that, eight years after, that is, in the thirty-fifth of that reign, a complete and not ill proportioned representation by counties and boroughs was bestowed upon Wales by Act of Parliament. From that moment, as by a charm, the tumults subsided; obedience was restored; peace, order, and civilization followed in the train of liberty. When the day-star of the English Constitution had arisen in their hearts, all was harmony within and without —

> " — simul alba nautis
>   Stella refulsit,
> Defluit saxis agitatus humor;
> Concidunt venti, fugiuntque nubes,
> Et minax (quod sic voluere) ponto
>   Unda recumbit."

The very same year the County Palatine of Chester received the same relief from its oppressions and the same remedy to its disorders. Before this time Chester was little less distempered than Wales. The inhabitants, without rights themselves, were the fittest to destroy the rights of others; and from thence Richard the Second drew the standing army of archers with which for a time he oppressed England. The people of Chester applied to Parliament in a petition penned as I shall read to you:

5 "To the King, our Sovereign Lord, in most humble wise shewen unto your excellent Majesty the inhabitants of your Grace's County Palatine of Chester: (1) That where the said County Palatine of Chester is and hath been always hitherto exempt, excluded, and separated out and
10 from your High Court of Parliament, to have any Knights and Burgesses within the said Court; by reason whereof the said inhabitants have hitherto sustained manifold disherisons, losses, and damages, as well in their lands, goods, and bodies, as in the good, civil, and politic govern-
15 ance and maintenance of the commonwealth of their said county; (2) And forasmuch as the said inhabitants have always hitherto been bound by the Acts and Statutes made and ordained by your said Highness and your most noble progenitors, by authority of the said Court, as far forth
20 as other counties, cities, and boroughs have been, that have had their Knights and Burgesses within your said Court of Parliament, and yet have had neither Knight ne Burgess there for the said County Palatine; the said inhabitants, for lack thereof, have been oftentimes touched and
25 grieved with Acts and Statutes made within the said Court, as well derogatory unto the most ancient jurisdictions, liberties, and privileges of your said County Palatine, as prejudicial unto the commonwealth, quietness, rest, and peace of your Grace's most bounden subjects inhabiting
30 within the same."

What did Parliament with this audacious address? — Reject it as a libel? Treat it as an affront to Government? Spurn it as a derogation from the rights of legislature? Did they toss it over the table? Did they
35 burn it by the hands of the common hangman? — They took the petition of grievance, all rugged as it was, without softening or temperament, unpurged of the original

bitterness and indignation of complaint — they made it the very preamble to their Act of redress, and consecrated its principle to all ages in the sanctuary of legislation.

Here is my third example. It was attended with the success of the two former. Chester, civilized as well as Wales, has demonstrated that freedom, and not servitude, is the cure of anarchy; as religion, and not atheism, is the true remedy for superstition. Sir, this pattern of Chester was followed in the reign of Charles the Second with regard to the County Palatine of Durham, which is my fourth example. This county had long lain out of the pale of free legislation. So scrupulously was the example of Chester followed that the style of the preamble is nearly the same with that of the Chester Act; and, without affecting the abstract extent of the authority of Parliament, it recognizes the equity of not suffering any considerable district in which the British subjects may act as a body, to be taxed without their own voice in the grant.

Now if the doctrines of policy contained in these preambles, and the force of these examples in the Acts of Parliaments, avail anything, what can be said against applying them with regard to America? Are not the people of America as much Englishmen as the Welsh? The preamble of the Act of Henry the Eighth says the Welsh speak a language no way resembling that of his Majesty's English subjects. Are the Americans not as numerous? If we may trust the learned and accurate Judge Barrington's account of North Wales, and take that as a standard to measure the rest, there is no comparison. The people cannot amount to above 200,000; not a tenth part of the number in the Colonies. Is America in rebellion? Wales was hardly ever free from it. Have you attempted to govern America by penal statutes? You made fifteen for Wales. But your legislative authority is perfect with regard to America. Was it less perfect in Wales, Chester, and Durham? But America is virtually represented. What! does the electric force of virtual representation more easily pass over the Atlantic than pervade Wales, which lies in your neighborhood — or than Chester and Durham, surrounded by abundance of representation that is actual and palpable? But, Sir, your ancestors thought this sort of virtual representation, however ample, to be totally insufficient for the freedom of the inhabitants of territories that are so near, and comparatively so inconsiderable. How then can I think it sufficient for those which are infinitely greater, and infinitely more remote?

You will now, Sir, perhaps imagine that I am on the point of proposing to you a scheme for a representation of the Colonies in Parliament. Perhaps I might be inclined to entertain some such thought; but a great flood stops me in my course. *Opposuit natura.* — I cannot remove the eternal barriers of the creation. The thing, in that mode, I do not know to be possible. As I meddle with no theory, I do not absolutely assert the impracticability of such a representation; but I do not see my way to it, and those who have been more confident have not been more successful. However, the arm of public benevolence is not shortened, and there are often several means to the same end. What nature has disjoined in one way, wisdom may unite in another. When we cannot give the benefit as we would wish, let us not refuse it altogether. If we cannot give the principal, let us find a substitute. But how? Where? What substitute?

Fortunately I am not obliged, for the ways and means of this substitute, to tax my own unproductive invention. I am not even obliged to go to the rich treasury of the fertile framers of imaginary commonwealths — not to the Republic of Plato, not to the Utopia of More, not to the Oceana of Harrington. It is before me — it is at my feet,

"And the rude swain
Treads daily on it with his clouted shoon."

I only wish you to recognize, for the theory, the ancient constitutional policy of this kingdom with regard to representation, as that policy has been declared in Acts of Parliament; and as to the practice, to return to that mode which a uniform experience has marked out to you as best, and in which you walked with security, advantage, and honor, until the year 1763.

My Resolutions therefore mean to establish the equity and justice of a taxation of America by *grant*, and not by *imposition;* to mark the *legal competency* of the Colony Assemblies for the support of their government in peace, and for public aids in time of war; to acknowledge that this legal competency has had a *dutiful and beneficial exercise;* and that experience has shown the *benefit of their grants,* and the *futility of Parliamentary taxation* as a method of supply.

These solid truths compose six fundamental propositions. There are three more Resolutions corollary to these. If you admit the first set, you can hardly reject the others. But if you admit the first, I shall be far from solicitous whether you accept or refuse the last. I think these six massive pillars will be of strength sufficient to support the temple of British concord. I have no more doubt than I entertain of my existence that, if you admitted these, you would command an immediate peace, and, with but tolerable future management, a lasting obedience in America. I am not arrogant in this confident assurance. The propositions are all mere matters of fact, and if they are such facts as draw irresistible conclusions even in the stating, this is the power of truth, and not any management of mine.

Sir, I shall open the whole plan to you, together with such observations on the motions as may tend to illustrate them where they may want explanation. The first is a Resolution —

> "That the Colonies and Plantations of Great Britain in North America, consisting of fourteen separate Governments, and containing two millions and upwards of free inhabitants, have not had the liberty and privilege of electing and sending any Knights and Burgesses, or others, to represent them in the High Court of Parliament."

This is a plain matter of fact, necessary to be laid down, and, excepting the description, it is laid down in the language of the Constitution; it is taken nearly *verbatim* from acts of Parliament.

The second is like unto the first —

> "That the said Colonies and Plantations have been liable to, and bounden by, several subsidies, payments, rates, and taxes given and granted by Parliament, though the said Colonies and Plantations have not their Knights and Burgesses in the said High Court of Parliament, of their own election, to represent the condition of their country; by lack whereof they have been oftentimes touched and grieved by subsidies given, granted, and assented to, in the said Court, in a manner prejudicial to the commonwealth, quietness, rest, and peace of the subjects inhabiting within the same."

Is this description too hot, or too cold; too strong, or too weak? Does it arrogate too much to the supreme legislature? Does it lean too much to the claims of the people? If it runs into any of these errors, the fault is not mine. It is the language of your own ancient Acts of Parliament.

> "Non meus hic sermo, sed quæ præcepit Ofellus,
> Rusticus, abnormis sapiens."

It is the genuine produce of the ancient, rustic, manly, homebred sense of this country. — I did not dare to rub off a particle of the venerable rust that rather adorns and preserves, than destroys, the metal. It would be a profanation to touch with a tool the stones which constuct the sacred altar of peace. I would not violate with modern polish the ingenuous and noble roughness of these truly Constitutional materials. Above all things, I was resolved not to be guilty of tampering, the odious vice of restless and unstable minds. I put my foot in the tracks of our forefathers, where I can neither wander nor stumble. Determining to fix articles of peace, I was resolved not to be wise beyond what was written; I was resolved to use nothing else than the form of sound words, to let others abound in their own sense, and carefully to abstain from all expressions of my own. What the law has said, I say. In all things else I am silent. I have no organ but for her words. This, if it be not ingenious, I am sure is safe.

There are indeed words expressive of grievance in this second Resolution, which those who are resolved always to be in the right will deny to contain matter of fact, as applied to the present case, although Parliament thought them true with regard to the counties of Chester and Durham. They will deny that the Americans were ever "touched and grieved" with the taxes. If they consider nothing in taxes but their weight as pecuniary impositions, there might be some pretence for this denial; but men may be sorely touched and deeply grieved in their privileges, as well as in their purses. Men may lose little in property by the act which takes away all their freedom. When a man is robbed of a trifle on the highway, it is not the two-pence lost that constitutes the capital outrage. This is not confined to privileges. Even ancient indulgences, withdrawn without offence on the part of those who enjoyed such favors, operate as grievances. But were the Americans then not touched and grieved by the taxes, in some measure, merely as taxes? If so, why were they almost all either wholly repealed, or exceedingly reduced? Were they not touched and grieved even by the regulating duties of the sixth of George the Second? Else, why were the duties first reduced to one third in 1764, and afterwards to a third of that third in the year 1766? Were they not touched and grieved by the Stamp Act? I shall say they were, until that tax is revived. Were they not touched and grieved by the duties of 1767, which were likewise repealed, and which Lord Hillsborough tells you, for the Ministry, were laid contrary to the true principle of commerce? Is not the assurance given by that noble person to the Colonies of a resolution to lay no more taxes on them an admission that taxes would touch and grieve them? Is not the Resolution of the noble lord in the blue ribbon, now standing on your Journals, the strongest of all proofs that Parliamentary subsidies really touched and grieved them? Else why all these changes, modifications, repeals, assurances, and resolutions?

The next proposition is —

"That, from the distance of the said Colonies, and from other circumstances, no method hath hitherto been devised for procuring a representation in Parliament for the said Colonies."

This is an assertion of a fact. I go no further on the paper, though, in my private judgment, a useful representation is impossible — I am sure it is not desired by them, nor ought it perhaps by us — but I abstain from opinions.

The fourth Resolution is —

"That each of the said Colonies hath within itself a body, chosen in part, or in the whole, by the freemen, freeholders, or other free inhabitants thereof, commonly called the General Assembly, or General Court, with powers legally to raise, levy, and assess, according to the several usage of such Colonies, duties and taxes towards defraying all sorts of public services."

This competence in the Colony Assemblies is certain. It is proved by the whole tenor of their Acts of Supply in all the Assemblies, in which the constant style of granting is, "an aid to his Majesty;" and Acts granting to the Crown have regularly for near a century passed the public offices without dispute. Those who have been pleased paradoxically to deny this right, holding that none but the British Parliament can grant to the Crown, are wished to look to what is done, not only in the Colonies, but in Ireland, in one uniform unbroken tenor every session. Sir, I am surprised that this doctrine should come from some of the law servants of the Crown. I say that if the Crown could be responsible, His Majesty — but certainly the Ministers, — and even these law officers themselves through whose hands the Acts passed, biennially in Ireland, or annually in the Colonies — are in an habitual course of committing impeachable offences. What habitual offenders have been all Presidents of the Council, all Secretaries of State, all First Lords of Trade, all Attorneys and all Solicitors-General! However, they are safe, as no one impeaches them; and there is no ground of charge against them except in their own unfounded theories.

The fifth resolution is also a resolution of fact —

"That the said General Assemblies, General Courts, or other bodies legally qualified as aforesaid, have at sundry times freely granted several large subsidies and public aids for his Majesty's service, according to their abilities, when required thereto by letter from one of his Majesty's principal Secretaries of State; and that their right to grant the same, and their cheerfulness and sufficiency in the said grants, have been at sundry times acknowledged by Parliament."

To say nothing of their great expenses in the Indian wars, and not to take their exertion in foreign ones so high as the supplies in the year 1695 — not to go back to their public contributions in the year 1710 — I shall begin to travel only where the journals give me light, resolving to deal in nothing but fact, authenticated by Parliamentary record, and to build myself wholly on that solid basis.

On the 4th of April, 1748, a Committee of this House came to the following resolution:

> "Resolved: That it is the opinion of this Committee that it is just and reasonable that the several Provinces and Colonies of Massachusetts Bay, New Hampshire, Connecticut, and Rhode Island, be reimbursed the expenses they have been at in taking and securing to the Crown of Great Britain the Island of Cape Breton and its dependencies."

The expenses were immense for such Colonies. They were above £200,000 sterling; money first raised and advanced on their public credit.

On the 28th of January, 1756, a message from the King came to us, to this effect:

> "His Majesty, being sensible of the zeal and vigor with which his faithful subjects of certain Colonies in North America have exerted themselves in defence of his Majesty's just rights and possessions, recommends it to this House to take the same into their consideration, and to enable his Majesty to give them such assistance as may be a proper reward and encouragement."

On the 3d of February, 1756, the House came to a suitable Resolution, expressed in words nearly the same as those of the message, but with the further addition, that the money then voted was as an encouragement to the Colonies to exert themselves with vigor. It will not be necessary to go through all the testimonies which your own records have given to the truth of my Resolutions. I will only refer you to the places in the Journals:

    Vol. xxvii. — 16th and 19th May, 1757.
    Vol. xxviii. — June 1st, 1758; April 26th and 30th, 1759; March 26th and 31st, and April 28th, 1760; Jan. 9th and 20th, 1761.
    Vol. xxix. — Jan. 22d and 26th, 1762; March 14th and 17th, 1763.

Sir, here is the repeated acknowledgment of Parliament that the Colonies not only gave, but gave to satiety. This nation has formally acknowledged two things: first, that the Colonies had gone beyond their abilities, Parliament having thought it necessary to reimburse them; secondly, that they had acted legally and laudably in their grants of money, and their maintenance of troops, since the compensation is expressly given as reward and encouragement. Reward is not bestowed for acts that are unlawful; and encouragement is not held out to things that deserve reprehension. My Resolution therefore does nothing more than collect into one proposition what is scattered through your Journals. I give you nothing but your own; and you cannot refuse in the gross what you have so often acknowledged in detail. The admission of this, which will be so honorable to them and to you, will, indeed, be mortal to all the miserable stories by which the passions of the misguided people have been engaged in an unhappy system. The people heard, indeed, from the beginning of these disputes, one thing continually dinned in their ears, that reason and justice demanded that the Americans, who paid no taxes, should be compelled to contribute. How did that fact of their paying nothing stand when the taxing system began? When Mr. Grenville began to form his system of American revenue, he stated in this

House that the Colonies were then in debt two millions six hundred thousand pounds sterling money, and was of opinion they would discharge that debt in four years. On this state, those untaxed people were actually subject to the payment of taxes to the amount of six hundred and fifty thousand a year. In fact, however, Mr. Grenville was mistaken. The funds given for sinking the debt did not prove quite so ample as both the Colonies and he expected. The calculation was too sanguine; the reduction was not completed till some years after, and at different times in different Colonies. However, the taxes after the war continued too great to bear any addition, with prudence or propriety; and when the burthens imposed in consequence of former requisitions were discharged, our tone became too high to resort again to requisition. No Colony, since that time, ever has had any requisition whatsoever made to it.

We see the sense of the Crown, and the sense of Parliament, on the productive nature of a *revenue by grant*. Now search the same Journals for the produce of the *revenue by imposition*. Where is it? Let us know the volume and the page. What is the gross, what is the net produce? To what service is it applied? How have you appropriated its surplus? What! Can none of the many skilful index-makers that we are now employing find any trace of it? — Well, let them and that rest together. But are the Journals, which say nothing of the revenue, as silent on the discontent? Oh no! a child may find it. It is the melancholy burthen and blot of every page.

I think, then, I am, from those Journals, justified in the sixth and last Resolution, which is —

"That it hath been found by experience that the manner of granting the said supplies and aids, by the said General Assemblies, hath been more agreeable to the said Colonies,

and more beneficial and conducive to the public service,
than the mode of giving and granting aids in Parliament,
to be raised and paid in the said Colonies."

This makes the whole of the fundamental part of the
plan. The conclusion is irresistible. You cannot say
that you were driven by any necessity to an exercise of
the utmost rights of legislature. You cannot assert that
you took on yourselves the task of imposing Colony taxes
from the want of another legal body that is competent
to the purpose of supplying the exigencies of the state
without wounding the prejudices of the people. Neither
is it true that the body so qualified, and having that
competence, had neglected the duty.

The question now, on all this accumulated matter, is:
whether you will choose to abide by a profitable experience, or a mischievous theory; whether you choose to
build on imagination, or fact; whether you prefer enjoyment, or hope; satisfaction in your subjects, or discontent?

If these propositions are accepted, everything which
has been made to enforce a contrary system must, I take
it for granted, fall along with it. On that ground, I have
drawn the following Resolution, which, when it comes to
be moved, will naturally be divided in a proper manner:

> "That it may be proper to repeal an Act made in the seventh
> year of the reign of his present Majesty, entitled, An Act
> for granting certain duties in the British Colonies and Plantations in America; for allowing a drawback of the duties
> of customs upon the exportation from this Kingdom of
> coffee and cocoa-nuts of the produce of the said Colonies or
> Plantations; for discontinuing the drawbacks payable on
> china earthenware exported to America; and for more
> effectually preventing the clandestine running of goods in
> the said Colonies and Plantations. And that it may be
> proper to repeal an Act made in the fourteenth year of the
> reign of his present Majesty, entitled, An Act to discon-

tinue, in such manner and for such time as are therein mentioned, the landing and discharging, lading or shipping of goods, wares, and merchandise at the town and within the harbor of Boston, in the Province of Massachusetts Bay, in North America. And that it may be proper to repeal an Act made in the fourteenth year of the reign of his present Majesty, intitled, An Act for the impartial administration of justice in the cases of persons questioned for any acts done by them in the execution of the law, or for the suppression of riots and tumults, in the Province of Massachusetts Bay, in New England. And that it may be proper to repeal an Act made in the fourteenth year of the reign of his present Majesty, intitled, An Act for the better regulating of the Government of the Province of the Massachusetts Bay, in New England. And also that it may be proper to explain and amend an Act made in the thirty-fifth year of the reign of King Henry the Eighth, intitled, An Act for the Trial of Treasons committed out of the King's Dominions."

I wish, Sir, to repeal the Boston Port Bill, because — independently of the dangerous precedent of suspending the rights of the subject during the King's pleasure — it was passed, as I apprehend, with less regularity and on more partial principles than it ought. The corporation of Boston was not heard before it was condemned. Other towns, full as guilty as she was, have not had their ports blocked up. Even the Restraining Bill of the present session does not go to the length of the Boston Port Act. The same ideas of prudence which induced you not to extend equal punishment to equal guilt, even when you were punishing, induced me, who mean not to chastise, but to reconcile, to be satisfied with the punishment already partially inflicted.

Ideas of prudence and accommodation to circumstances prevent you from taking away the charters of Connecticut and Rhode Island, as you have taken away that of Massachusetts Bay, though the Crown has far less power in the two former provinces than it enjoyed in the latter, and though the abuses have been full as great, and as flagrant, in the exempted as in the punished. The same reasons of prudence and accommodation have weight with me in restoring the Charter of Massachusetts Bay. Besides, Sir, the Act which changes the charter of Massachusetts is in many particulars so exceptionable that if I did not wish absolutely to repeal, I would by all means desire to alter it, as several of its provisions tend to the subversion of all public and private justice. Such, among others, is the power in the Governor to change the sheriff at his pleasure, and to make a new returning officer for every special cause. It is shameful to behold such a regulation standing among English laws.

The Act for bringing persons accused of committing murder, under the orders of Government to England for trial, is but temporary. That Act has calculated the probable duration of our quarrel with the Colonies, and is accommodated to that supposed duration. I would hasten the happy moment of reconciliation, and therefore must, on my principle, get rid of that most justly obnoxious Act.

The Act of Henry the Eighth, for the Trial of Treasons, I do not mean to take away, but to confine it to its proper bounds and original intention; to make it expressly for trial of treasons — and the greatest treasons may be committed — in places where the jurisdiction of the Crown does not extend.

Having guarded the privileges of local legislature, I would next secure to the Colonies a fair and unbiassed judicature, for which purpose, Sir, I propose the following Resolution:

> "That, from the time when the General Assembly or General Court of any Colony or Plantation in North America shall have appointed by Act of Assembly, duly confirmed, a settled salary to the offices of the Chief Justice and other

Judges of the Superior Court, it may be proper that the said Chief Justice and other Judges of the Superior Courts of such Colony shall hold his and their office and offices during their good behavior, and shall not be removed therefrom but when the said removal shall be adjudged by his Majesty in Council, upon a hearing on complaint from the General Assembly, or on a complaint from the Governor, or Council, or the House of Representatives severally, or of the Colony in which the said Chief Justice and other Judges have exercised the said offices."

The next Resolution relates to the Courts of Admiralty. It is this:

"That it may be proper to regulate the Courts of Admiralty or Vice-Admiralty authorized by the fifteenth Chapter of the Fourth of George the Third, in such a manner as to make the same more commodious to those who sue, or are sued, in the said Courts, and to provide for the more decent maintenance of the Judges in the same."

These courts I do not wish to take away; they are in themselves proper establishments. This court is one of the capital securities of the Act of Navigation. The extent of its jurisdiction, indeed, has been increased, but this is altogether as proper, and is indeed on many accounts more eligible, where new powers were wanted, than a court absolutely new. But courts incommodiously situated, in effect, deny justice; and a court partaking in the fruits of its own condemnation is a robber. The Congress complain, and complain justly, of this grievance.

These are the three consequential propositions. I have thought of two or three more, but they come rather too near detail, and to the province of executive government, which I wish Parliament always to superintend, never to assume. If the first six are granted, congruity will carry the latter three. If not, the things that remain unrepealed will be, I hope, rather unseemly incumbrances on the building, than very materially detrimental to its strength and stability.

Here, Sir, I should close; but I plainly perceive some objections remain which I ought, if possible, to remove. The first will be that, in resorting to the doctrine of our ancestors, as contained in the preamble to the Chester Act, I prove too much; that the grievance from a want of representation, stated in that preamble, goes to the whole of legislation as well as to taxation; and that the Colonies, grounding themselves upon that doctrine, will apply it to all parts of legislative authority.

To this objection, with all possible deference and humility, and wishing as little as any man living to impair the smallest particle of our supreme authority, I answer, that the words are the words of Parliament, and not mine, and that all false and inconclusive inferences drawn from them are not mine, for I heartily disclaim any such inference. I have chosen the words of an Act of Parliament which Mr. Grenville, surely a tolerably zealous and very judicious advocate for the sovereignty of Parliament, formerly moved to have read at your table in confirmation of his tenets. It is true that Lord Chatham considered these preambles as declaring strongly in favor of his opinions. He was a no less powerful advocate for the privileges of the Americans. Ought I not from hence to presume that these preambles are as favorable as possible to both, when properly understood; favorable both to the rights of Parliament, and to the privilege of the dependencies of this Crown? But, Sir, the object of grievance in my Resolution I have not taken from the Chester, but from the Durham Act, which confines the hardship of want of representation to the case of subsidies, and which therefore falls in exactly with the case of the Colonies. But whether the unrepresented counties were *de jure* or *de facto* bound, the preambles do not accurately distinguish, nor indeed was it necessary; for, whether *de jure* or *de facto*, the Legislature thought the exercise of the power of taxing as of right, or as of fact without right, equally a grievance, and equally oppressive.

I do not know that the Colonies have, in any general way, or in any cool hour, gone much beyond the demand of humanity in relation to taxes. It is not fair to judge of the temper or dispositions of any man, or any set of men, when they are composed and at rest, from their conduct or their expressions in a state of disturbance and irritation. It is besides a very great mistake to imagine that mankind follow up practically any speculative principle, either of government or of freedom, as far as it will go in argument and logical illation. We Englishmen stop very short of the principles upon which we support any given part of our Constitution, or even the whole of it together. I could easily, if I had not already tired you, give you very striking and convincing instances of it. This is nothing but what is natural and proper. All government, indeed every human benefit and enjoyment, every virtue, and every prudent act, is founded on compromise and barter. We balance inconveniences; we give and take; we remit some rights, that we may enjoy others; and we choose rather to be happy citizens than subtle disputants. As we must give away some natural liberty to enjoy civil advantages, so we must sacrifice some civil liberties for the advantages to be derived from the communion and fellowship of a great empire. But, in all fair dealings, the thing bought must bear some proportion to the purchase paid. None will barter away the immediate jewel of his soul. Though a great house is apt to make slaves haughty, yet it is purchasing a part of the artificial importance of a great empire too dear to pay for it all essential rights and all the intrinsic dignity of human nature. None of us who would not risk his life rather than fall under a government purely arbitrary. But although there are some amongst us who think our Constitution wants many improvements to make it a complete system of liberty, perhaps none who are of that opinion would think it right to aim at such improvement by disturbing his country, and risking everything that is dear to him. In every arduous enterprise we consider what we are to lose, as well as what we are to gain; and the more and better stake of liberty every people possess, the less they will hazard in a vain attempt to make it more. These are the cords of man. Man acts from adequate motives relative to his interest, and not on metaphysical speculations. Aristotle, the great master of reasoning, cautions us, and with great weight and propriety, against this species of delusive geometrical accuracy in moral arguments as the most fallacious of all sophistry.

The Americans will have no interest contrary to the grandeur and glory of England, when they are not oppressed by the weight of it; and they will rather be inclined to respect the acts of a superintending legislature when they see them the acts of that power which is itself the security, not the rival, of their secondary importance. In this assurance my mind most perfectly acquiesces, and I confess I feel not the least alarm from the discontents which are to arise from putting people at their ease, nor do I apprehend the destruction of this Empire from giving, by an act of free grace and indulgence, to two millions of my fellow-citizens some share of those rights upon which I have always been taught to value myself.

It is said, indeed, that this power of granting, vested in American Assemblies, would dissolve the unity of the

Empire, which was preserved entire, although Wales, and Chester, and Durham were added to it. Truly, Mr. Speaker, I do not know what this unity means, nor has it ever been heard of, that I know, in the constitutional
5 policy of this country. The very idea of subordination of parts excludes this notion of simple and undivided unity. England is the head; but she is not the head and the members too. Ireland has ever had from the beginning a separate, but not an independent, legisla-
10 ture, which, far from distracting, promoted the union of the whole. Everything was sweetly and harmoniously disposed through both islands for the conservation of English dominion, and the communication of English liberties. I do not see that the same principles might
15 not be carried into twenty islands and with the same good effect. This is my model with regard to America, as far as the internal circumstances of the two countries are the same. I know no other unity of this Empire than I can draw from its example during these periods,
20 when it seemed to my poor understanding more united than it is now, or than it is likely to be by the present methods.

But since I speak of these methods, I recollect, Mr. Speaker, almost too late, that I promised, before I fin-
25 ished, to say something of the proposition of the noble lord on the floor, which has been so lately received and stands on your Journals. I must be deeply concerned whenever it is my misfortune to continue a difference with the majority of this House; but as the reasons for
30 that difference are my apology for thus troubling you, suffer me to state them in a very few words. I shall compress them into as small a body as I possibly can, having already debated that matter at large when the question was before the Committee.

35 First, then, I cannot admit that proposition of a ran-

som by auction; because it is a mere project. It is a thing new, unheard of; supported by no experience; justified by no analogy; without example of our ancestors, or root in the Constitution. It is neither regular Parliamentary taxation, nor Colony grant. *Experimentum in corpore vili* is a good rule, which will ever make me adverse to any trial of experiments on what is certainly the most valuable of all subjects, the peace of this Empire.

Secondly, it is an experiment which must be fatal in the end to our Constitution. For what is it but a scheme for taxing the Colonies in the ante-chamber of the noble lord and his successors? To settle the quotas and proportions in this House is clearly impossible. You, Sir, may flatter yourself you shall sit a state auctioneer, with your hammer in your hand, and knock down to each Colony as it bids. But to settle, on the plan laid down by the noble lord, the true proportional payment for four or five and twenty governments according to the absolute and the relative wealth of each, and according to the British proportion of wealth and burthen, is a wild and chimerical notion. This new taxation must therefore come in by the back door of the Constitution. Each quota must be brought to this House ready formed; you can neither add nor alter. You must register it. You can do nothing further; for on what grounds can you deliberate either before or after the proposition? You cannot hear the counsel for all these provinces, quarrelling each on its own quantity of payment, and its proportion to others. If you should attempt it, the Committee of Provincial Ways and Means, or by whatever other name it will delight to be called, must swallow up all the time of Parliament.

Thirdly, it does not give satisfaction to the complaint of the Colonies. They complain that they are taxed

without their consent; you answer, that you will fix the
sum at which they shall be taxed. That is, you give
them the very grievance for the remedy. You tell them,
indeed, that you will leave the mode to themselves. I
really beg pardon — it gives me pain to mention it —
but you must be sensible that you will not perform this
part of the compact. For, suppose the Colonies were to
lay the duties, which furnished their contingent, upon
the importation of your manufactures, you know you
would never suffer such a tax to be laid. You know,
too, that you would not suffer many other modes of taxation; so that, when you come to explain yourself, it will
be found that you will neither leave to themselves the
quantum nor the mode, nor indeed anything. The whole
is delusion from one end to the other.

Fourthly, this method of ransom by auction, unless it
be universally accepted, will plunge you into great and
inextricable difficulties. In what year of our Lord are
the proportions of payments to be settled? To say
nothing of the impossibility that Colony agents should
have general powers of taxing the Colonies at their dis-
cretion, consider, I implore you, that the communication
by special messages and orders between these agents and
their constituents, on each variation of the case, when
the parties come to contend together and to dispute on
their relative proportions, will be a matter of delay, per-
plexity, and confusion that never can have an end.

If all the Colonies do not appear at the outcry, what
is the condition of those assemblies who offer, by themselves or their agents, to tax themselves up to your ideas
of their proportion? The refractory Colonies who refuse
all composition will remain taxed only to your old impositions, which, however grievous in principle, are trifling as to production. The obedient Colonies in this
scheme are heavily taxed; the refractory remain un-

burdened. What will you do? Will you lay new and heavier taxes by Parliament on the disobedient? Pray consider in what way you can do it. You are perfectly convinced that, in the way of taxing, you can do nothing but at the ports. Now suppose it is Virginia that refuses to appear at your auction, while Maryland and North Carolina bid handsomely for their ransom, and are taxed to your quota, how will you put these Colonies on a par? Will you tax the tobacco of Virginia? If you do, you give its death-wound to your English revenue at home, and to one of the very greatest articles of your own foreign trade. If you tax the import of that rebellious Colony, what do you tax but your own manufactures, or the goods of some other obedient and already well-taxed Colony? Who has said one word on this labyrinth of detail, which bewilders you more and more as you enter into it? Who has presented, who can present you with a clue to lead you out of it? I think, Sir, it is impossible that you should not recollect that the Colony bounds are so implicated in one another — you know it by your other experiments in the bill for prohibiting the New England fishery,—that you can lay no possible restraints on almost any of them which may not be presently eluded, if you do not confound the innocent with the guilty, and burthen those whom, upon every principle, you ought to exonerate. He must be grossly ignorant of America who thinks that, without falling into this confusion of all rules of equity and policy, you can restrain any single Colony, especially Virginia and Maryland, the central and most important of them all.

Let it also be considered that, either in the present confusion you settle a permanent contingent, which will and must be trifling, and then you have no effectual revenue; or you change the quota at every exigency, and then on every new repartition you will have a new quarrel.

Reflect, besides, that when you have fixed a quota for every Colony, you have not provided for prompt and punctual payment. Suppose one, two, five, ten years' arrears. You cannot issue a Treasury Extent against the failing Colony. You must make new Boston Port Bills, new restraining laws, new acts for dragging men to England for trial. You must send out new fleets, new armies. All is to begin again. From this day forward the Empire is never to know an hour's tranquillity. An intestine fire will be kept alive in the bowels of the Colonies, which one time or other must consume this whole Empire. I allow indeed that the empire of Germany raises her revenue and her troops by quotas and contingents; but the revenue of the empire, and the army of the empire, is the worst revenue and the worst army in the world.

Instead of a standing revenue, you will therefore have a perpetual quarrel. Indeed, the noble lord who proposed this project of a ransom by auction seems himself to be of that opinion. His project was rather designed for breaking the union of the Colonies than for establishing a revenue. He confessed he apprehended that his proposal would not be to their taste. I say this scheme of disunion seems to be at the bottom of the project; for I will not suspect that the noble lord meant nothing but merely to delude the nation by an airy phantom which he never intended to realize. But whatever his views may be, as I propose the peace and union of the Colonies as the very foundation of my plan, it cannot accord with one whose foundation is perpetual discord.

Compare the two. This I offer to give you is plain and simple. The other full of perplexed and intricate mazes. This is mild; that harsh. This is found by experience effectual for its purposes; the other is a new project. This is universal; the other calculated for certain Colonies only. This is immediate in its conciliatory operation; the other remote, contingent, full of hazard. Mine is what becomes the dignity of a ruling people — gratuitous, unconditional, and not held out as a matter of bargain and sale. I have done my duty in proposing it to you. I have indeed tired you by a long discourse; but this is the misfortune of those to whose influence nothing will be conceded, and who must win every inch of their ground by argument. You have heard me with goodness. May you decide with wisdom! For my part, I feel my mind greatly disburthened by what I have done to-day. I have been the less fearful of trying your patience, because on this subject I mean to spare it altogether in future. I have this comfort, that in every stage of the American affairs I have steadily opposed the measures that have produced the confusion, and may bring on the destruction, of this Empire. I now go so far as to risk a proposal of my own. If I cannot give peace to my country, I give it to my conscience.

But what, says the financier, is peace to us without money? Your plan gives us no revenue. No! But it does; for it secures to the subject the power of refusal, the first of all revenues. Experience is a cheat, and fact a liar, if this power in the subject of proportioning his grant, or of not granting at all, has not been found the richest mine of revenue ever discovered by the skill or by the fortune of man. It does not indeed vote you 152,750*l.* 11*s.* 2¾*d.*, nor any other paltry limited sum; but it gives the strong box itself, the fund, the bank — from whence only revenues can arise amongst a people sensible of freedom. *Posita luditur arca.* Cannot you, in England — cannot you, at this time of day — cannot you, a House of Commons, trust to the principle which has raised so mighty a revenue, and accumulated a debt of near 140,000,000 in this country? Is this principle to

be true in England, and false everywhere else? Is it
not true in Ireland? Has it not hitherto been true in
the Colonies? Why should you presume that, in any
country, a body duly constituted for any function will
5 neglect to perform its duty and abdicate its trust? Such
a presumption would go against all governments in all
modes. But, in truth, this dread of penury of supply
from a free assembly has no foundation in nature; for
first, observe that, besides the desire which all men have
10 naturally of supporting the honor of their own government, that sense of dignity and that security to property
which ever attends freedom has a tendency to increase
the stock of the free community. Most may be taken
where most is accumulated. And what is the soil or
15 climate where experience has not uniformly proved that
the voluntary flow of heaped-up plenty, bursting from
the weight of its own rich luxuriance, has ever run with
a more copious stream of revenue than could be squeezed
from the dry husks of oppressed indigence by the strain-
20 ing of all the politic machinery in the world?

Next, we know that parties must ever exist in a free
country. We know, too, that the emulations of such
parties — their contradictions, their reciprocal necessi-
ties, their hopes, and their fears — must send them all
25 in their turns to him that holds the balance of the State.
The parties are the gamesters; but Government keeps
the table, and is sure to be the winner in the end. When
this game is played, I really think it is more to be feared
that the people will be exhausted, than that government
30 will not be supplied; whereas, whatever is got by acts
of absolute power ill obeyed, because odious, or by con-
tracts ill kept, because constrained, will be narrow, feeble,
uncertain, and precarious.

"Ease would retract
35 Vows made in pain, as violent and void."

I, for one, protest against compounding our demands. I declare against compounding, for a poor limited sum, the immense, ever-growing, eternal debt which is due to generous government from protected freedom. And so may I speed in the great object I propose to you, as I think it would not only be an act of injustice, but would be the worst economy in the world, to compel the Colonies to a sum certain, either in the way of ransom or in the way of compulsory compact.

But to clear up my ideas on this subject: a revenue from America transmitted hither — do not delude yourselves — you never can receive it; no, not a shilling. We have experience that from remote countries it is not to be expected. If, when you attempted to extract revenue from Bengal, you were obliged to return in loan what you had taken in imposition, what can you expect from North America? For certainly, if ever there was a country qualified to produce wealth, it is India; or an institution fit for the transmission, it is the East India Company. America has none of these aptitudes. If America gives you taxable objects on which you lay your duties here, and gives you, at the same time, a surplus by a foreign sale of her commodities to pay the duties on these objects which you tax at home, she has performed her part to the British revenue. But with regard to her own internal establishments, she may, I doubt not she will, contribute in moderation. I say in moderation, for she ought not to be permitted to exhaust herself. She ought to be reserved to a war, the weight of which, with the enemies that we are most likely to have, must be considerable in her quarter of the globe. There she may serve you, and serve you essentially.

For that service — for all service, whether of revenue, trade, or empire — my trust is in her interest in the British Constitution. My hold of the Colonies is in the

close affection which grows from common names, from kindred blood, from similar privileges, and equal protection. These are ties which, though light as air, are as strong as links of iron. Let the Colonists always keep
5 the idea of their civil rights associated with your government, — they will cling and grapple to you, and no force under heaven will be of power to tear them from their allegiance. But let it be once understood that your government may be one thing, and their privileges
10 another, that these two things may exist without any mutual relation, the cement is gone — the cohesion is loosened — and everything hastens to decay and dissolution. As long as you have the wisdom to keep the sovereign authority of this country as the sanctuary of
15 liberty, the sacred temple consecrated to our common faith, wherever the chosen race and sons of England worship freedom, they will turn their faces towards you. The more they multiply, the more friends you will have; the more ardently they love liberty, the more perfect
20 will be their obedience. Slavery they can have anywhere — it is a weed that grows in every soil. They may have it from Spain; they may have it from Prussia. But, until you become lost to all feeling of your true interest and your natural dignity, freedom they can have
25 from none but you. This is the commodity of price of which you have the monopoly. This is the true Act of Navigation which binds to you the commerce of the Colonies, and through them secures to you the wealth of the world. Deny them this participation of freedom,
30 and you break that sole bond which originally made, and must still preserve, the unity of the Empire. Do not entertain so weak an imagination as that your registers and your bonds, your affidavits and your sufferances, your cockets and your clearances, are what form the
35 great securities of your commerce. Do not dream that

your letters of office, and your instructions, and your
suspending clauses, are the things that hold together the
great contexture of the mysterious whole. These things
do not make your government. Dead instruments, passive tools as they are, it is the spirit of the English communion that gives all their life and efficacy to them. It
is the spirit of the English Constitution which, infused
through the mighty mass, pervades, feeds, unites, invig-
orates, vivifies every part of the Empire, even down to
the minutest member.

Is it not the same virtue which does everything for us
here in England? Do you imagine, then, that it is the
Land Tax Act which raises your revenue? that it is the
annual vote in the Committee of Supply which gives you
your army? or that it is the Mutiny Bill which inspires
it with bravery and discipline? No! surely no! It is
the love of the people; it is their attachment to their
government, from the sense of the deep stake they have
in such a glorious institution, which gives you your army
and your navy, and infuses into both that liberal obedience without which your army would be a base rabble,
and your navy nothing but rotten timber.

All this, I know well enough, will sound wild and
chimerical to the profane herd of those vulgar and me-
chanical politicians who have no place among us; a sort
of people who think that nothing exists but what is gross
and material, and who, therefore, far from being qualified
to be directors of the great movement of empire, are not
fit to turn a wheel in the machine. But to men truly
initiated and rightly taught, these ruling and master
principles which, in the opinion of such men as I have
mentioned, have no substantial existence, are in truth
everything, and all in all. Magnanimity in politics is
not seldom the truest wisdom; and a great empire and
little minds go ill together. If we are conscious of our

station, and glow with zeal to fill our places as becomes our situation and ourselves, we ought to auspicate all our public proceedings on America with the old warning of the church, *Sursum corda!* We ought to elevate our
5 minds to the greatness of that trust to which the order of providence has called us. By adverting to the dignity of this high calling our ancestors have turned a savage wilderness into a glorious empire, and have made the most extensive and the only honorable conquests — not
10 by destroying, but by promoting the wealth, the number, the happiness, of the human race. Let us get an American revenue as we have got an American empire. English privileges have made it all that it is; English privileges alone will make it all it can be.
15 In full confidence of this unalterable truth, I now, *quod felix faustumque sit,* lay the first stone of the Temple of Peace; and I move you —

> "That the Colonies and Plantations of Great Britain in North America, consisting of fourteen separate governments, and
20 containing two millions and upwards of free inhabitants, have not had the liberty and privilege of electing and sending any Knights and Burgesses, or others, to represent them in the High Court of Parliament."

NOTES.

THE ENGLISH CONSTITUTION AND GOVERNMENT.

The English speeches contained in this volume make frequent reference to a structure of government and to forms and usages unlike those with which we are familiar in the United States. Information upon these subjects is absolutely necessary to an intelligent reading of these speeches, and yet it is not always readily accessible. It has therefore been thought best to embody in succinct statement the peculiar features of the English Constitution, government, and procedure touched upon in the speeches, and incidentally to point out the pitfalls which lurk under the guise of terms and expressions similar in form to our own, but different in content and meaning. It should be noted that the point of view in the following sketch is that of the present status in England. Historical differences within the period covered will be noticed as they occur in the speeches themselves.

THE BRITISH CONSTITUTION.

When a new organization of government was adopted and put upon trial in the United States in 1789, the special features of that organization were set forth in a well-known document, which, by a natural transfer of meaning, took the name of the order and organization which it described; that is, the Constitution of the United States of America. Ever since that time the extraordinary interest centring in this document has, in the usage of American speakers and writers, tended steadily to shift the meaning of the word Constitution to this narrower base; that is, from the actual order and organization of government to the document in which that order is officially described and promulgated. This limitation of meaning is by no means prevalent outside the realm of American politics; and the young American student should be specially cautioned against interpreting in any such narrow sense the frequent reference made by Englishmen to the British Constitution. England has no written Constitution; nor, under the circumstances, could she well have one. Her government is the outcome of ages of experiment and struggle; of incessant re-adjustment of conflicting powers and interests; sometimes of sharp and decisive action; more frequently of insensible but irresistible drifting upon the current of national tendency. Questions of constitutionality, therefore, are settled in England, not by appeal to a state-paper like ours, since none exists, but by appeal to unchallenged usage, to precedents not reversed, or to legislation not repealed, wherever these are to be found in the centuries between Magna Charta and the present time. Even in cases where we find citation of what is claimed to be the very language of the Constitution, we are not to understand anything more than that the language is that of *some* document of acknowledged authority in determining usage; as, for example, an Act of Parliament. And the English Constitution is altered, not through the formality of an amendment voted upon by the people, but by embodying the innovation directly in legislative act,—subject, of course, to prompt ratification or rejection by the people in their next return of members to Parliament. To Englishmen, then, the Constitution means primarily *the established order of government*, whether this be (1) with reference to its organization, its actual structure, and the relation of its parts; or (2) with reference to usage, precedent, and law; or (3) with reference to its genius and spirit. In the first sense the word is often loosely synonymous with our use of the word government; but for this last word English usage has developed a special meaning (see below), which excludes it in certain connections. Examples of these several uses of the word may be found on p. 257, l. 32; p. 50, l. 15; p. 79, l. 35; and p. 42, l. 25.

THE CABINET.

In England the executive power, as of old, is vested nominally in the Crown, but really in the Cabinet, or Ministry, with which body the sovereign is associated, both as its honorary head and as a permanent councillor; influential indeed, but without vote, responsibility, or place in its sessions. Whenever a decisive change of party or of policy becomes apparent in the votes of the House of Commons, the old Cabinet resigns, and a new one is formed to put the new policy into operation. Theoretically the Queen is free to choose whom she will to become Prime Minister and form the new Cabinet; but practically the choice is limited to a single person, the acknowledged leader of the party which has become uppermost in the Commons. The Prime Minister selects his colleagues from among the ablest men of his party and its allies in both Houses, a significant feature of the scheme being the fact that the Ministers are actually members of Parliament, are present at its sessions, and play a most important part in its deliberations. The Cabinet so constituted is, therefore, a committee of the majority. But it is more than this. It is a committee "with power," charged with the duty of acting in momentous affairs, and often without previous consultation with Parliament. Upon it devolves, furthermore, nearly the whole initiative in legislation, — the duty of planning, introducing, and bringing to decision almost all measures discussed in Parliament. The promptness and completeness with which this body of men is vested with imperial power, in every realm save that of the Judiciary, is startling indeed to American ideas. The Ministry becomes at once both heart and brain of the government, and during its tenure of office wields a power far transcending that of our Presidential Administration. A sufficient safeguard against abuse of this power is found in the immediate responsibility of the Ministry to the Commons; that is, in the swiftness and certainty of its downfall if it fails to carry the majority with it. Out of the feeling that the Ministry is the vital centre of government, Englishmen have come to call it "Her Majesty's Government," "the Government," or simply "Government." In these expressions there is often an implied reference to that other equally important and equally recognized part of the system, "the Opposition;" that is, the organized minority, in its character of critic and advocate for the other side, charged with the duty of allowing nothing to pass without challenge and efficient scrutiny.

PARLIAMENT.

The Parliament of England consists of two bodies, or "Houses," the Lords and the Commons. The House of Lords stands for the conservatism of ancient privilege; the Commons, for the final sovereignty of the people. The one is for the most part hereditary, and often continues without radical change during long periods of time; the other is the direct representative of the people, and is kept such by frequent general elections. Parliament assembles at the summons of the Crown; that is, of the Ministry in the name of the Queen. It is opened by a Speech from the Throne read in the House of Lords. Its annual session is usually from February to August, at the close of which it is "prorogued" by the Crown; and in the end it is dissolved by the same authority. The term of a Parliament is really the term of the Lower House, since that alone is affected by elections. Its utmost possible term is fixed by statute at seven years; but no Parliament of modern times has survived so long. Dissolution of Parliament comes about at no stated time, but rather as an exigency of government. When the Ministers find themselves confronted by an adverse majority in the Commons, if issue is clearly joined and the majority decisive, they are expected to resign their power at once into the hands of the majority. But if there is doubt as to whether this majority really represents the will of the people, the Ministry may dissolve Parliament and "go to the country"—that is, appeal to the people upon the issue raised.

THE HOUSE OF LORDS.

The House of Lords has a membership of over five hundred, consisting of the following groups: (1) The Lords Temporal; i.e., the hereditary peerage of England with a small representation chosen from the peerage of Scotland and of Ireland. (2) The Lords Spiritual; i.e., the higher clergy of the Established Church, in the persons of the archbishops and bishops. (3) The higher judiciary, in the persons of the Lord Chancellor and three distinguished lawyers or judges designated by the Crown, and called Lords of Appeal in Ordinary, or, more popularly, "Law Lords."

These three groups are separately addressed in Chatham's speech, p. 87. The Lord Chancellor presides, and is a member of the regnant ministry; the Law Lords are advisers of the Lords upon legal matters. These persons, however, are not by virtue of their offices "lords of Parliament," — members entitled to speak and to vote in the ordinary business of the Upper House. Even the Chancellor's seat, the famous "woolsack," is theoretically outside the precincts of the Lords, although it is, in fact, almost in the centre of their chamber. But in recent practice the Chancellor is regularly made an hereditary peer, if he is not one already, and the Law Lords are made peers for life. Only a mere fraction of the membership is ordinarily found in attendance upon business. Three members, it is said, constitute a quorum; and, until recently, members might vote by proxy without being present or hearing discussion. In legislation, the House of Lords is theoretically of equal weight with the House of Commons, since the consent of both is requisite to the passage of any Act. But, in reality, the power of the former has greatly dwindled, partly because of what is felt to be the narrowness of its sympathy and interest outside of its own class; still more because of its exclusion from the great field of finance and taxation; and, most of all, because in the end it can always be forced to assent to the will of the Commons by the simple expedient of having new peers created by the Ministry in the name of the Crown, and thus overwhelming the adverse majority. The fear that such action would be taken was sufficient to secure the assent of the Lords to the Reform Bill of 1832; — a sufficient number of the majority, though bitterly opposed to the bill, deliberately absented themselves to avoid precipitating the crisis. The influence of the peerage upon legislation is still great in many ways; but the actual power of their House in a contested case is limited to a power of cautious revision and a veto to stay proceedings until the people shall have spoken again, and with decisive emphasis, upon the point in question.

It should be noted in passing, that the House of Lords has judicial functions in which its action is quite independent of the Commons. It sits as a Court of Impeachment in cases like that of **Warren Hastings,** and as a court for the trial of members of its own order charged with treason or felony. Furthermore, it sits, — or, as we should say, a committee consisting only of its legal members sits, — as a Supreme Court of Appeals for the kingdom.

THE HOUSE OF COMMONS.

As the result of successive changes in the representation of the realm, the House of Commons now numbers six hundred and seventy members. The constituencies which "return" these members are either rural — counties and subdivisions of counties; urban — boroughs and wards; or universities. On receipt of the writ, or order for an election, the "returning officer" of each constituency arranges the preliminaries and fixes a date before which all candidates must announce themselves. When that date is reached, if no more candidates appear than there are seats to be filled, the candidates are "returned" by the officer — are reported as duly elected — without further formality of balloting. If, however, a seat is "contested" by two or more candidates, the officer appoints a day for "taking the poll." In general elections, therefore, it comes about that the polls are not taken in all the constituencies on the same day, but are scattered over a considerable interval of time. Thus, in a hotly contested campaign it not infrequently happens that some distinguished party champion attempts in the first instance to carry some stronghold of the enemy, is defeated there, and yet saves his place in Parliament by offering himself at the eleventh hour as a candidate in one of these later elections. Any fully qualified citizen not a member of the House of Lords, an officer of government, nor a clergyman either of the Established or Roman Church, may "stand;" i.e., is eligible to Parliament. Residence outside of the district is no bar, as we have seen above. The candidate not only pays all the expenses of his canvass, but must render a sworn statement of every item of it. If successful, he is free thereafter to serve the public in Parliament at his own expense, for the government allows him no compensation whatever. Only in very rare cases does a constituency volunteer to maintain in Parliament a member too poor to maintain himself. If the member becomes distinguished enough to be sought for high political office, such as a place in the Cabinet, he must, by submitting to a second election, obtain from his constituency permission to serve them in the double capacity of member and minister.

The old Houses of Parliament, in which Burke, Chatham, and Macaulay spoke, were destroyed by fire in 1834. Their essential features, arrangements, and usages, however, have all been repeated in the new Houses; and these will require some brief notice in view of the frequent reference made to them in the speeches. The "House" in which the Commons sit, and in which is transacted the business of the British Empire, is an oblong chamber surrounded by lobbies. At one end, on an elevated platform, is the Speaker's Chair. At a table below and in front of him sit the Clerks; beyond them lies the Mace, emblem of the Speaker's authority. Parallel with the sides and with the further end of the room are arranged the members' seats, tier above tier, filling the whole space with the exception of a narrow, oblong portion of open floor in the centre. From this open space the main aisle runs down the centre of the chamber; while an aisle at right angles to this, and known as the "gangway," intersects the side benches. There are three well-known groups of sittings: The front row of seats on the Speaker's right is called the Treasury Bench, and is occupied by the Ministers. Behind these are ranged the supporters of the Government — the members of the dominant party. The seats on the Speaker's left, and directly facing these last, are the Opposition Benches, occupied by the leaders and body of "Her Majesty's Opposition." The "cross-benches" at the end of the room, directly facing the Speaker, are the place for members who do not affiliate with either of the great parties. One's location in the House is thus an indication of his political relationships. No member, however, can claim exclusive right to any particular seat, since the sittings are far fewer than the membership. There are regularly five sessions a week; four of these run from 4 o'clock P.M. till late at night — sometimes till after day-break — and one, on Wednesday, from midday till 6 o'clock P.M. Members sit with their hats on, but remove them when they rise to speak.

The "House" of the Lords is in the same building with that

of the Commons, but at the further end of the corridor. Its general arrangements are not unlike those of the other chamber, save that the Speaker's seat — the woolsack — is moved forward toward the centre to make place for a raised platform and the royal throne at the end of the room.

FORMS OF PROCEDURE.

At the opening of Parliament the Commons, headed by their Speaker, attend at the bar[1] of the Lords to listen to the Speech from the Throne, a paper prepared, of course, by the Ministry, and resembling somewhat, in its general scope, our President's Message. At the close of the Speech they retire to their chamber, and, first of all, go through the form of reading some unimportant bill, in order to assert once more their right to deliberate freely about whatever they will, even though matters urged upon them by the Crown have to wait. Some member previously designated for this duty then moves the "Address" — the formal reply to the royal Speech, couched in subservient language, and strictly echoing the tone and the suggestions of that paper. In the debate which follows, there is a general airing of views of all sorts, and not infrequently amendments are proposed sharply criticising the acts or the policy of Government.[2] These matters disposed of, the regular business of the session begins. Of this there is inevitably an enormous amount, since many matters which in our country never come before Congress, but belong either to State, or to county, or to municipal government, are in England directly under the control of Parliament. But there is no such deluge of proposed legislation as that which greets us Americans at the opening of Congress. The House of Lords, as we have seen, does very little in initiating measures; while individual members of the Commons may introduce bills but sparingly, not as of right, but only by consent of the House. Furthermore, only the Wednesday afternoon

---

[1] A movable barrier or rail in the main aisle of each House, beyond which none but officers and members are allowed to pass.

[2] A debate upon a similar Address in the House of Lords was the occasion of Chatham's speech printed in this volume, and of an amendment proposed by him.

session of each week is available for the consideration of business so introduced. The Ministry is held responsible for the introduction of all necessary legislation; while the duty of the House is primarily to scrutinize, discuss, amend, accept, or reject the measures the Ministry proposes. Government measures have, therefore, large right of way; three full sessions each week are devoted to them exclusively. Questions propounded to the Ministry form a noteworthy feature of the Parliamentary scheme, affording, as they do, to the House an admirable means of informing itself on matters it needs to know, and to the Ministers an opportunity of directly stating their case and explaining their action. But neither measures nor questions may be sprung upon the House unawares. Full notice and precise statement of each must in all cases be previously given.

The regular course through which a Bill must pass to become a a law is as follows: The Bill, having been drafted, printed, and properly endorsed, comes to its "first reading," after due notice given and motion passed "for leave to bring in the Bill." Its title then is read aloud by the Clerk, and a motion is made that the Bill be read a second time on a future day named. When the day arrives, the proposer moves its second reading, and enters into a full explanation and defence of its provisions. Debate follows; and if the House consents to the second reading, it is understood as accepting the general principle of the measure, though not committing itself to the details. If the House refuses, the Bill is of course defeated. This second reading is therefore the most critical stage of a Bill in its course in the Commons, and calls for the most strenuous efforts of its defenders. After its second reading, the House votes to consider it in detail in a Committee on some future day named. In this Committee changes and amendments are agreed upon, and the Committee rises and reports to the House the Bill, usually in its final shape. The House orders its third reading, again in the future; and when this is reached, the motion is put "that the Bill be passed." Votes in the House are taken first *viva voce;* but if the result is doubted, a "division" is taken in this way: Those voting "Ay" pass out of the chamber into the lobby on the Speaker's right, while those voting "No" pass into the lobby on the left, until the Speaker remains alone. The members are counted as they file back into the chamber, and the result is announced. A Bill that successfully passes this stage is sent up to the Lords. If the Lords accept it, it receives, as a matter of course, the royal assent,[1] and becomes a law. If the Lords amend it, it must return to the Commons for their concurrence in the amendments. If the Lords "throw it out," or if the Commons refuse to accept the amendments of the Lords, the Bill, of course, is lost.

FINANCE AND TAXATION.

The principle that a free people must be free to tax itself and to spend its money as it will, is a principle which our fathers brought with them from the old country. The difference between a tax "given and granted" to the Crown by the people themselves, and a tax imposed by the Crown upon the people, was in the last century, to Englishmen on both sides of the Atlantic, a very vital difference — the difference between freedom and subjugation. Burke speaks of this point on p. 49, l. 13-21; and the whole subject is eloquently set forth by him in a speech upon American Taxation, not included in this volume. Out of this very matter grew our Revolutionary War. Since that war, however, there has been for us neither Crown nor subject, nor any participant in our government other than the people itself; and the old distinction is lost. Our governments of all degrees regularly levy, or impose, taxes; and the form of expression no longer awakes our wrath. But in England the old distinction and the old usage still hold. There the vast framework of government — outside of the Commons — has absolutely no vital or sustaining power within itself; it can levy no tax, can raise no revenue for its own support, has no income at all save what the people from year to year through their representatives, the Commons, actually "give and grant." The Queen, in her Speech from the Throne, must each year ask anew that "her faithful Commons" vote her the

---

[1] There was once a veto power resident in the Sovereign, but it is now practically lost. The Queen *must* assent to whatever passes the two Houses. The last veto in English history was by Queen Anne.

supplies without which every wheel in the system must come to a standstill. The Commons hold the purse. One of the chief matters, therefore, in the annual business of the House, is the consideration of the "Budget." The minister in charge of the finances of the realm is termed the Chancellor of the Exchequer. His most arduous duty is the preparation of estimates of expenditure for the coming year, and plans for taxation whereby the necessary amount may be raised. When this Budget is ready, the House receives and considers it in a "Committee of Supply." This is a Committee of the whole House, formed for the purpose of securing the utmost freedom of question and discussion, which would otherwise be hampered by strict parliamentary rules. The Speaker leaves his seat, the Mace is carried away, some member is made Chairman, and discussion runs on with little heed to the formality of rules. In this Committee is settled the amount Commons will grant the Crown, and the ends to which it is to be applied. This done, the same body resolves itself into a Committee of Ways and Means, to determine in like manner how the money shall be raised. When this Committee has closed its deliberations, it rises, the Speaker resumes his place, and the Chairman of the Committees reports to the House the conclusions reached, which are then embodied in a motion and passed by the House in its formal capacity. When a "Money Bill" has duly passed all its stages in the Commons, it is sent to the Lords, who have no power to alter or amend it, though they may reject it — if they dare. Furthermore, such a bill does not go up to the Queen along with others through the hands of the Lords, but is returned to the Commons, and at the end of the session is presented to her by the Speaker in person, as the gift of the people alone. And on such an occasion the Queen never fails to thank the Commons for their generosity.

In the preparation of the foregoing sketch the author has consulted among others the following works, and would recommend them to the student for further study or reference :

A Primer of the English Constitution and Government, by Sheldon Amos (Longmans, Green & Co., N.Y.) — a compact topical statement, with good Index and Appendices.

The English Constitution, by Walter Bagehot (Chapman, Hall & Co., London) — a brilliant and popular discussion of its excellences and defects.

The State, by Woodrow Wilson (D. C. Heath & Co., Boston) — specially valuable as a topical digest and manual of the structure and organization of all the great constitutional governments of the modern world.

The Law of the Constitution, a series of lectures by A. V. Dicey (Macmillan & Co.) — giving with utmost logical clearness the lawyer's view of the English Constitution, and explaining some of its principal maxims.

EDMUND BURKE.

EDMUND BURKE was born in Dublin, Ireland, in January, 1729. His father was an attorney with a fair practice, and looked forward to the same profession for his son. The boy received his education first in a private school; then in Trinity College, Dublin, — where he took the bachelor's degree in his nineteenth year; and last of all, in the Middle Temple, London. His studies gained him at the time no special academic honors, and never brought him to the actual practice of the law; yet in them, and especially in the wide and profound reading which accompanied them, was laid the foundation of his future greatness.

Burke's first public venture was in literature. In 1756 appeared his *Vindication of Natural Society* — a clever bit of irony — and his *Inquiry into the Origin of Our Ideas of the Sublime and the Beautiful*, an essay which at once attracted attention both in England and upon the Continent. Meantime, however, he had discovered the true bent of his genius, and was diligently studying the governmental problems of England. The first fruit of this study appeared in 1757, in his *Account of English Settlements in America*. From about this time also dates his long friendship with Dr. Johnson and the members of his famous Literary Club.

His political career began in 1765, when he became private secretary to Lord Rockingham, the head of the new Whig Ministry. A little later he was returned to Parliament as member for Wendover, taking his seat in time to distinguish himself in the debates which preceded the repeal of the Stamp Act in 1766. His career in Parliament lasted without break from this time until 1794, when, broken in health and spirits, he withdrew from public life. His death occurred not long after, in 1797.

A passion for order and a passion for justice, some one has said, were the master-motives of Burke's thought and life. Both these passions led him directly into that field of human activity where they find their noblest play, the field of practical government. During his lifetime three mighty questions successively confronted the government of England: (1) How shall a great nation deal with colonies of its own proud blood and free traditions? (2) How shall such a nation treat subject provinces of alien race and temper? (3) How shall it meet the fierce spirit of change and revolution at its very doors? They were the questions of America, of India, and of France. Into their discussion Burke threw himself with all the ardor and force of his great nature. In his utterance upon the first of these questions Burke was undoubtedly at his best. It is not merely that this topic is one which naturally attracts American readers. It is not merely that his arguments have still a living interest in their application to great questions which confront England in our own day. Burke brought to it a fresher, truer insight, a judgment more sane, a temper more serene and genial, than he was able to command later, after years spent in unavailing struggle and bitter conflict. Furthermore, this question raised no schism within himself. His passion for the established order and his passion for justice both led him to the same conclusion.

When the American Colonies were forever lost, Burke turned his attention to the government of England's East Indian possessions. A series of brilliant speeches in Parliament led up to his crowning effort upon this subject, the speech at the trial of Warren Hastings, in 1787. Burke's grasp of facts is now more masterful, and his oratory more splendid than ever; but the noble effect is somewhat marred by a shrillness of tone, an excitement of personal feeling, and a fierceness of invective from which his earlier utterances were free.

In 1789 came the crash of the French Revolution. Burke's horror at the overthrow of long-established order was so great as to leave no room for calm consideration of justice as between oppressor and oppressed. With fiercer and fiercer outcry from this time onward he urged England to espouse the cause of the old tyranny, and to put down the Revolution.

SPEECH ON CONCILIATION WITH THE COLONIES.

At the opening of the year 1775 the harsh treatment which the Colonies were receiving from England had forced them to combine for mutual support against further aggression. The Continental Congress had already assembled. Lexington and Bunker Hill were not far off. It was becoming a matter of grave importance to the English government to break up this formidable union, and to bring the Colonies once more to deal separately and singly with England. At this juncture Lord North, the Prime Minister, unexpectedly announced what he was pleased to term a measure for "conciliating the differences with America." He proposed to exempt from further taxation any Colony which, after providing for the maintenance of its own government, should guarantee to the mother-country an amount satisfactory to her as being, "according to the condition, circumstances, and situation of such Colony," its proportionate contribution toward the common defence. This transparent scheme deceived no one, — it was really a plan to divide and conquer. To the friends of the Colonies, however, it was no small thing that the Ministry, after a long policy of coercion, should not merely accept, but of its own accord announce, the principle of conciliation. Burke seized the opportunity to propose conciliation which might really be effective.

TEXTUAL NOTES.

PAGE 1, 1. **the austerity of the Chair** means, of course, 'the dignity and seriousness of this assembly.' The parliamentary fiction which regards not merely the dignity, but the personality, of the House as embodied in its Speaker, is an old-time device to banish from public deliberations the fierceness and the confusion of personal encounters. To it we owe our common rule of debate that all remarks must be addressed to the Chair, and that no mention be made by name of any person in the assembly. This rule was, no doubt, more rigidly observed in Burke's day than it is at present. But the literalness with which Burke at times carries out the fiction, though meant as pleasantry, has a strong dash of the grotesque; as it has here in his ascription to the Chair of the actual moods and temper of the members, and again on p. 9, l. 3, 4, where with doubtful compliment he speaks of "a blunter discernment than yours." In a like vein is his disparagement here of his own perfectly natural and worthy feeling as 'frailty' and 'superstition.' Burke's weighty genius is not always at its best in toying with trifles.

8. **the grand penal bill** was a measure of Lord North's, cutting off the New England colonies from all trade except with the mother country and her dependencies, and, worst of all, putting a stop to the fisheries, one of their most successful and important industries. See pp. 14-16. The Lords returned the bill with a savage amendment making it apply to *all* the American Colonies. The amendment was afterwards withdrawn.

PAGE **2**, 6, 7. This was at the beginning of 1766. Long before this date, however, Burke had discerned the gravity of the Colonial question, and had with characteristic energy set himself to master it; as is shown by his *Account of European Settlements in America*, published in 1757.

25, 26. The occasion was a memorable one — the repeal of the Stamp Act under Lord Rockingham's Ministry, March 18, 1766. The strength and sharpness of the impression made upon Burke are attested by a striking passage in his speech upon American Taxation, wherein, after sketching the situation within the House on that night, and the bearing of the great leaders there, he goes on to tell how, outside the walls of the chamber, "the whole trading interest of this Empire, crammed into your lobbies, with a trembling and anxious expectation waited, almost to a winter's return of light, their fate from your resolutions;" and how, when the result was announced, "from the whole of that grave multitude there arose an involuntary burst of gratitude and transport."

PAGE **3**. 15-17. This was a Mr. Rose Fuller, now in the Opposition along with Burke. During the previous session it was his proposition to repeal the Tea Tax which furnished the occasion of Burke's famous speech upon American Taxation, referred to in the last note.

Page 4, 12-19. Upon the Ministry and its supporters, Burke means to say, rests the responsibility for devising schemes for carrying on government. Schemes proposed by the Opposition are not merely sure to receive no fair consideration from the triumphant majority, but are apt thereby to be discredited in advance, and ruined for future usefulness. The scruple is thoroughly characteristic of Burke, as are also the considerations which induced him to set it aside.

Page 6, 9-14. the project has been outlined above in the Introductory Note to this speech. The impossibility of assigning any definite values to the factors which were to determine the proportionate share of each Colony, as well as the cool irony of talking about proportion at all, when the real object was in each case to extort the largest sum possible, strongly roused Burke. His imagination at once pictures the scenes Parliament is likely to witness in attempting to carry out such a scheme, and he sarcastically figures these as the splendors and sensations of a new entertainment provided by the Ministry. **The noble lord** was Frederick North, Prime Minister from 1770 till 1782, and largely responsible for the separation of the Colonies from England. He was at this time 'lord' only by courtesy of speech. He did not come into his earldom until his father's death in 1790. Sons and younger brothers of peers, though commonly styled lords, are only commoners in fact, and as such are eligible to the lower house, where they often seek a career. A notable example in our own day is Lord Randolph Churchill. The **blue ribbon** is the badge of the famous Order of the Garter, a decoration rarely conferred upon commoners, and therefore often mentioned by Burke in his parliamentary designation of this Prime Minister to whom he was so long opposed.

Colony agents. In default of any regular channel through which a colony could make its condition and its needs known to Parliament, the practice was to secure the services of some member of Parliament to act as agent for the colony, and to look after its interests in the general legislation. Burke himself was such an agent for New York. A fuller recognition is now accorded the colonies of England, in the addition to the Ministry of a special Secretary of State for the Colonies. But the Agents-General are still maintained. **the interposition of your mace.** When the ordinary call for order is ineffective to quell disturbance in the House, the Sergeant-at-Arms, at the Speaker's direction, takes up the mace from the table where it lies, and with it confronts the disorderly members. Before this symbol of the majesty of the House, they are expected to quail and sink into their seats. There is in the Speaker's power but one last resource more dreaded than this, and that is to "name" the disorderly member.

25, 26. For **the Address** see Note on the English Constitution, page 322. Its **menacing front** in this case was the declaration of a state of rebellion in Massachusetts, and a call for immediate action to suppress it. One of the **heavy bills of pains and penalties** was that referred to in the opening sentences of this speech as "the grand penal bill." See note, p. 1, l. 8.

PAGE **9**, 5–12. An **occasional system** here means a policy which lacks the guidance of far-reaching principles, and so contents itself with makeshifts to meet new occasions or emergencies as they arise—a policy of shifts. The **object** referred to in l. 6 and 12, and repeatedly throughout this discussion, is the Colonies themselves.

22. That is, 'the subject of their commerce has been treated,' etc. The gentleman was a Mr. Glover, who presented a petition from the West India planters praying that peace might be made with the American Colonies. His literary reputation, complimented here, is now quite forgotten. The **bar** is a movable barrier or rail in the main aisle, beyond which none but officers and members are allowed to pass. All other persons, if permitted to address the House, must do so standing outside this barrier.

PAGE **10**, 9. **state**, where we should say **statement**. See also p. 56, l. 4.

21–23. The exports from England to Africa consisted almost wholly of articles used in barter for slaves, who were shipped thence to the Colonies. The exchange on the coast of Africa was but an incident in a larger transaction beginning in England and ending in America. The amount of these exports is, therefore, rightly added by Burke to the total of direct exports to the Colonies.

PAGE 12, 10 ff. To secure a more vivid sense of the unexampled vigor and growth of the Colonies than mere statistics could give, Burke pauses here to turn upon the subject the gorgeous illumination of this paragraph. The attempt is a daring one, and is carried out with characteristic opulence and splendor. The good taste of portions of it has been questioned; particularly the academic and conventional fulsomeness of lines 24–35; but that would hardly have counted as a fault in a century which admired such displays.

22, 23. 'Already old enough to read the deeds of his fathers, and able to know what virtue is;' — adapted from Virgil, Ecl. iv. 26.

27–35. the fourth generation, since George III., was, not the son, but the grandson of George II. **made Great Britain** by the union with Scotland in 1707. The **higher rank of peerage** was that of Earl, to which Lord Bathurst had been advanced from that of Baron, the lowest hereditary degree. The new title added to the honors of the family was that of Baron Apsley, conferred upon Lord Bathurst's son when the latter became Lord Chancellor.

PAGE 14, 10. deceive, i.e., *beguile, lighten,* — an echo of Latin usage in the case of the parallel word, *fallere.*

27–29. Alluding to the famous story of a Roman father condemned to die of starvation, but secretly nourished by his daughter from her own breasts, until the discovery of her devotion and the admiration it aroused brought about his release.

PAGE 15, 11. The **Serpent,** — a constellation within the Antartic circle.

17. run the longitude. This expression seems not to be current with nautical men; although they naturally interpret it as spoken of a course sailed due east or west, so that the ship's progress is reckoned in longitude alone. On the other hand, the context seems to call for a course due south, or nearly so — following a great circle of longitude, or meridian. It may be that Burke has used the phrase here strictly, as the sailors understand it; **meaning** that some of the American whalers, after their

African cruise, sailed westward to Brazil, as perhaps they might do on their homeward cruise. Or it may be that without strict question of nautical interpretation he used the sonorous phrase in the other sense, which seemed obvious enough to him.

PAGE **16**, 10. **complexion**, in its original signification of *temperament*, the way in which a person is 'put together;' and so generally in Burke. Passages like that which follows here (pp. 16, 17) justify Matthew Arnold's high praise of Burke, "because almost alone in England he brings thought to bear upon politics; he saturates politics with thought."

PAGE **18**, 9, 10. During the great struggle against the tyranny of the Stuarts.

21-24. Notably in Rome, an example always present to Burke's mind. PAYNE.

PAGE **19**, 27-29. **popular**, democratic, 'of the people and by the people.' **merely popular**,—wholly so. **the popular representative** the portion which represents the people. Cf. Burke's more explicit statement, p. 52, l. 34 ff.

31. **aversion** is now followed by *to*, after the manner of its synonyms, *dislike*, *repugnance*, etc. But in Burke's time the force of a Latin etymology or of Latin usage was still strongly felt, and often determined both idiom and meaning of English words. Hence the *from* in this case. The young student, whose sense for idiom and usage needs to grow more sure and more intelligent, should not fail to notice these cases as they arise. Even though unacquainted with Latin, he should lose no time in acquiring the habit of consulting directly the Latin Lexicon. With a little resolution and a little help at first, the difficulties will speedily vanish; while the gain in conscious power and in grasp of language is invaluable. For examples at hand try *piety*, p. 14, l. 27, *communion*, p. 20, l. 27, and *constitution*, p. 22, l. 21.

PAGE **21**, 29-31. This high and jealous spirit of the free-born in Rome in the midst of a servile class may be illustrated from almost any page of Shakespeare's *Julius Cæsar*. Our Teutonic and Scandinavian ancestry was habitually, though incorrectly, called Gothic by writers of the last century. **such were the Poles**, for at this time they had ceased to be an independent nation.

PAGE 22, 6, 7. The lead seems still to be held by the lawyers. The law is still considered to be the most natural avenue to a political career.

12. **Plantations**—colonies, the *plantings* of a new society or race. The term is regularly so used in acts and charters, and has no reference whatever to cultivation of the soil.

18–21. In the hope of paralyzing all concerted action on the part of the colonists, an order was issued forbidding the calling of town-meetings after Aug. 1, 1774. But a way was soon found, and within the limit of the law, to *hold* such meetings without calling them. The last called meeting before that date was simply *adjourned* to whatever time was thought desirable, and its legal existence was thus prolonged indefinitely.

25, 26. This was Thurlow, a famous lawyer, and afterwards Lord Chancellor. At this time he was Attorney-General, and a conspicuous figure among the Ministers on the Treasury Bench. Directly in front of him was the narrow space of open floor; hence, the designation of his position as "on the floor." To guard its freedom of speech, the House of Commons in earlier times used its utmost powers to prevent any attempt at reporting its debates. It thus became, and still is, a grave breach of decorum for a member to use pencil and paper in the House at all, unless it were to make a brief note of a point to which he would reply. Burke thus understands Thurlow's note-book and pencil, and avails himself of the unusual action to identify, without naming him, the person he means.

32. "Studies pass over into character," or "What we pursue takes shape again in our life;" a famous aphorism from Ovid, Heroid. Ep. xv. 83, quoted also by Bacon in his essay *Of Studies*.

PAGE 23, 15–17. A splendid figure developed out of Horace's fine phrase in the opening of one of his Odes (Bk. iv. 4), comparing Drusus in his victorious career to Jove's eagle, "the thunder's winged minister," *ministrum fulminis alitem*.

PAGE 24, 26, 27. **with all its imperfections on its head.** Adapted from the words of the ghost in *Hamlet*, Act I., Scene v. 79.

PAGE 30, 8. "To the despoiled are still left arms."—JUVENAL, *Sat.* viii. 124.

26. Cf. Acts xix. 19.

33. **more chargeable,** involving heavier charge, more expensive.

PAGE 31, 35, 36. Quoted from that treasury of bathos, *The Art of Sinking in Poetry,* ch. xi. The remote source of the lines in "one of Dryden's plays," though affirmed by various editors, seems to lack verification.

PAGE 32, 26, 27. **Sir Edward Coke,** a famous lawyer under Elizabeth and James; Attorney-General in 1603, when Raleigh was tried for treason. "While the prisoner defended himself with the calmest dignity and self-possession, Coke burst into the bitterest invective, brutally addressing the great courtier, as if he were a servant, in the phrase long remembered for its insolence and injustice, 'Thou hast an English face, but a Spanish heart!'" —*Encyc. Brit.*

PAGE 33, 14, 15. *ex vi termini*—by the very nature of the expression.

PAGE 34, 29. **addressed**—petitioned the Crown in an Address. Cf. Note on Forms of Procedure, p. 322.

PAGE 36, 7. **startle,** intransitive, meaning *start.* Cf. Dictionary.

27–29. From *Paradise Lost*, II., 592–594.

PAGE 38, 12, 13. **American financiers**—financiers who would hope to raise a revenue by taxing America.

24. Mr. Rice.

34. **shall** tell you—'is bound to,' 'is sure to;' with fuller recognition than is now common of the original meaning of this auxiliary.

PAGE 39, 3. **Acts of Navigation,** passed first in 1651, re-enacted later, and repealed only within our own century. They were designed to secure to England a practical monopoly of the carrying trade by sea. According to them, no vessel of another realm might bring either to England or to her colonies anything except the actual products of that realm. Cf. Encyclopedia, s. v. Navigation Laws.

22, 23. the pamphlet, by Dean Tucker, somewhat famous in the discussions of this time, and noticed by Johnson, as well as by Burke in his previous speech on American Taxation.

PAGE **41, 30.** For a clear understanding of the various matters referred to in this paragraph, the student should consult some succinct sketch of the history of Ireland, such, for example, as may be found in Chambers's Encyclopedia; or, better still, with the help of the Index, the subject may be followed up in Green's *Short History of the English People*, a work which ought always to be within reach of the student of English Literature.

PAGE **42, 17. Sir John Davis,** or rather, Davies, "Speaker of the First Irish House of Commons in 1612." — PAYNE.

33–35. The two great crises which have occurred in the course of English constitutional history are the revolt of the Parliament against Charles I., and the revolution which brought in William and Mary and established the principle of ministerial responsibility to Parliament. The first is habitually called by Englishmen the Great Rebellion, and the other the Revolution. Their application of these terms must not be confounded with other applications more familiar to us.

PAGE **43, 3, 4.** Burke here goes much further than the facts with regard to Ireland warrant. Ireland has never been "a principal part of England's strength and name."

21. Cf. Green's *Short History*. The parallel between Ireland and Wales is close and cogent so far as concerns the era of repression and savage coercion in each. On the other hand, the difference in the remedial measures applied to the two, and the difference in the results, have furnished a powerful argument in the discussion of the Irish question since Burke's time. Many parts of this speech gather fresh significance when read in the light of recent English history.

33. as secondary — as deputy. The word is a noun here.

PAGE **45, 25–30.** From Horace, Odes, Book I. xii. 27, comparing the advent of Augustus upon the distracted world to the rising of Castor and Pollux (the constellation of Gemini), upon the stormy sea. "As soon as the bright star has flashed on the view of the sailors, the raging sea retires from the rocks, winds sink and clouds disperse, and on the open main — so they [the deities] have willed it — the threatening swell is laid."

PAGE 46, 6. **shewen**, the older spelling of *show* with the old English plural ending, identical with that of modern German.

PAGE 48, 19. "Nature has planted [a barrier] in the way."— JUVENAL, *Sat.* x. 152. The Latin poets and the English Bible fortunately were both familiar to Burke's audience, and one of the notable features of his oratory is the telling effect with which he marks his climaxes of thought by some pregnant text from these sources or from the English poets.

PAGE 49, 4, 5. From *Comus*, l. 634, 635, inexactly quoted.

28. **temple of British concord**, with obvious allusion to the Temple of Concord in Rome, in which the Senate met during the troublous times of Catiline's conspiracy. The richness and frequency of allusion in Burke far transcend the possibility of annotation, but they should not be overlooked by any one who would feel the force and charm of his writing. See, for example, the whole of the first paragraph on p. 51.

PAGE 50, 34, 35. "Not mine is this language, but what Ofellus taught me: rustic, but of wisdom not learned in schools."— HORACE, *Sat.* II. ii. 2, 3.

PAGE 55, 27, 28. **misguided people**, *sc.* of England. **engaged in**, enlisted in favor of.

PAGE 62, 33, 34. **the immediate jewel of his soul**, *Othello*, III. iii. 156. **A great house**, etc.— even slaves feel a pride in the glory of a princely establishment to which they belong, and are willing to sacrifice something for the distinction it confers upon them. A reminiscence from Juvenal, *Sat.* v. 66.

PAGE 64, 10, 11. Burke lived to see this state of things reversed, and to approve the abolition of a separate Irish legislature. — PAYNE.

PAGE 65, 5, 6. "Experiments should be tried on objects of no value."

PAGE 68, 4. **a Treasury Extent**, — a summary process of compelling the payment of debts due the Crown by seizure of persons, lands, and goods.

13. **empire of Germany**, — the so-called Holy Roman Empire,

already little more than a name in Burke's time, and formally brought to an end in 1806. Cf. Bryce's *Holy Roman Empire*.

PAGE **69, 31**. "The treasure-chest is staked on the game." — the utmost resources of the Colonies will thus be pledged to secure England's success. See p. 70, l. 21 ff.

PAGE **70, 34, 35**. *Paradise Lost*, iv., 96, 97, inexactly quoted.

PAGE **74, 3, 4**. **warning** in the old sense of summons or call. *Sursum corda*, "Lift up your hearts!" — the exhortation which, in all the old liturgies, as well as in the Prayer Book, prefaces the sacrament of the Communion.

15, 16. "Happy and auspicious may it prove!" — the old Roman invocation prefacing all high and solemn acts.

Burke's propositions, it will be noticed, are strictly resolutions, as he calls them. If passed, they would have been mere expressions of the views and opinions of the assembly, and not legislation proper in the form of an Act of Parliament. After the recital of circumstances (Resolutions 1–6), instead of an "enacting clause" to make that which follows law, we have in each section the words, "That it may be proper to." — In this way it was possible to bring these matters to discussion and to a vote; whereas legislation would at best have incurred many delays, and in this case, with the Ministry to oppose it at every step, it could hardly have been brought to the consideration of the House at all. (See Note on Forms of Procedure, p. 323.) Still, could these resolutions have passed, the Ministers would, in effect, have been instructed to introduce and forward the legislation indicated, or else to vacate their places.

This speech shared the fate which attended most of Burke's efforts. Its force and eloquence commanded universal admiration, but were powerless to bring about what he desired. The resolutions were lost by an overwhelming majority. What actually took place is stated in Hansard's *Parliamentary History* as follows:[1]

---

[1] The statement appended to the first edition of this speech, and copied by almost every editor since, that "upon this [first] Resolution the previous question was put *and carried*," is manifestly in error and absurd.

"Mr. Jenkinson moved the previous question upon the first Resolution. Upon this the House divided. . . . Yeas . . . 78, Noes, . . . 270. So it passed in the negative. The second, third, fourth and thirteenth Resolutions had also the previous question put on them. The others were negatived."

In American practice the motion "that the previous question be *now* put," is a well-known device to stop debate, and to force a vote on the main question pending before the assembly. It is made and seconded by persons who hope to carry first it, and then the main question immediately afterwards. If it fails, things are only as they were before. In England, on the contrary, the motion "that the previous question be put," is a device for killing the main question altogether, without coming to any direct vote upon it; is, in fact, a back-handed way of "tabling" it. The motion is made and seconded by persons who mean to vote against it; for, according to English theory, the assembly is not at liberty to consider further any question upon which it has decided that a vote shall not be taken. Thus, in the present instance, the Ministerial party used the "previous question" to get rid of Burke's troublesome array of facts without either admitting or denying them, and then voted down the policy he based upon those facts.

Introduction to Theme=Writing

By J. B. FLETCHER, Harvard University, and Professor G. R. CAR-
PENTER, Columbia College. 16mo, cloth, 136 pages. Price, 60 cents.

THE lectures that form the basis of this book were delivered by Mr. Fletcher before the Freshman class at Harvard College in the spring of 1893. These have been rearranged, with additional matter by Professor Carpenter. The result is a text-book for students who have completed the introductory course in rhetoric usually prescribed at the beginning of the Freshman year.

The fundamental idea of the book is that in practising any of the various kinds of composition the student must decide : —

1. Just what treatment will be most appropriate to the subject-matter in general.

2. What treatment will most clearly bring out his own individual ideas or impressions of this matter.

3. What treatment will make this subject most clear to the particular class of readers or hearers which he has in mind.

Letter-writing, Translation, Description, Criticism, Exposition, and Argument are each treated in a clear and concise manner, and exercises on each subject are freely introduced.

Professor John F. Genung, *in The School Review for September,* 1894: Instead of being directed to grind out these things (compositions), the student is here set at real literary tasks, forms of composition such as the best writers cultivate, methods that obtain in the highest enterprises of literature, ways of working such as, once mastered, will never cease to be practical. In this there is great advantage. If the student must "go through with the motions" of composition, as of course he must, there is great stimulus in his undertaking, from the outset, work that he may recognize as real, and that he may compare at every step with the literature of books and magazines.

Professor James W. Bright, *Johns Hopkins University:* The subject of the little treatise is handled with such admirable clearness and directness as to give it a genuine attractiveness which no teacher, and, it is to be hoped, few pupils, would fail to perceive.

Professor Fred N. Scott, *University of Michigan:* Theme-Writing is an admirable little work. It has a breadth of view and a charm of style that are often painfully absent from text-books in English. The book is well adapted to the needs of our students.

From Milton to Tennyson

Masterpieces of English Poetry. Edited by L. Du Pont Syle, University of California. 12mo, cloth, 480 pages. Price, $1.00.

IN this work the editor has endeavored to bring together within the compass of a moderate-sized volume as much narrative, descriptive, and lyric verse as a student may reasonably be required to read critically for entrance to college. From the nineteen poets represented, only such masterpieces have been selected as are within the range of the understanding and the sympathy of the high school student. Each masterpiece is given complete, except for pedagogical reasons in the cases of Thomson, Cowper, Byron, and Browning. Exigencies of space have compelled the editor reluctantly to omit Scott from this volume. The copyright laws, of course, exclude American poets from the scope of this work.

The low price of the book, together with its strong and attractive binding, make it especially desirable for those teachers who read with their classes even a small part of the poems it contains.

President D. S. Jordan, *Leland Stanford, Jr., University, Cal.:* I have received the copy of Mr. Syle's book, "From Milton to Tennyson," and have looked it over with a great deal of interest. It seems to be an excellent work for the purpose. The selections seem well adapted to high school use, and the notes are wisely chosen and well stated.

Professor Henry A. Beers, *Yale University:* The notes are helpful and suggestive. What is more, — and what is unusual in text-book annotations, — they are interesting and make very good reading; not at all schoolmasterish, but really literary in their taste and discernment of nice points.

Professor Elmer E. Wentworth, *Vassar College:* It is a most attractive book in appearance outward and inward, the selections satisfactory and just, the notes excellent. In schools where less time is given than in ours, no other book known to me, *me judice*, will be so good. I wish to commend the notes again.

Wm. E. Griffis, *Ithaca, N.Y.* The whole work shows independent research as well as refined taste and a repose of judgment that is admirable. The selected pieces are not overburdened with critical notes, while the suggestions for comparison and criticism, to be made by the student himself, are very valuable.

Paragraph=Writing

By Professor F. N. SCOTT, University of Michigan, and Professor J. V. DENNEY, Ohio State University. 12mo. 304 pages. Price, $1.00.

THE principles embodied in this work were developed and put in practice by its authors at the University of Michigan several years ago. Its aim is to make the paragraph the basis of a method of composition, and to present all the important facts of rhetoric in their application to it.

In Part I. the nature and laws of the paragraph are presented; the structure and function of the isolated paragraph are discussed, and considerable space is devoted to related paragraphs; that is, those which are combined into essays.

Part II. is a chapter on the theory of the paragraph intended for teachers and advanced students.

Part III. contains copious material for class work, selected paragraphs, suggestions to teachers, lists of subjects for compositions (about two thousand), and helpful references of many kinds.

The Revised Edition contains a chapter on the Rhetoric of the Paragraph, in which will be found applications of the paragraph-idea to the sentence, and to the constituent parts of the sentence, so far as these demand especial notice. The new material thus provided supplies, in the form of principles and illustrations, as much additional theory as the student of Elementary Rhetoric needs to master and apply, in order to improve the details of his paragraphs in unity, clearness, and force.

Professor J. M. Hart, *Cornell University:* The style of the writers is admirable for clearness and correctness. . . . They have produced an uncommonly sensible text-book. . . . For college work it will be hard to beat. I know of no other book at all comparable to it for freshman drill.

Professor Charles Mills Gayley, *University of California:* Paragraph-Writing is the best thing of its kind, — the only systematic and exhaustive effort to present a cardinal feature of rhetorical training to the educational world.

The Dial, *March,* 1894: Paragraph-Writing is one of the really practical books on English composition. . . . A book that successfully illustrates the three articles of the rhetorician's creed, — theory, example, and practice.

Select Essays of Macaulay

Edited by SAMUEL THURBER, Girls' High School, Boston. 12mo, 205 pages; cloth, 70 cents; boards, 50 cents.

THIS selection comprises the essays on Milton, Bunyan, Johnson, Goldsmith, and Madame D'Arblay, thus giving illustrations both of Macaulay's earlier and of his later style. It aims to put into the hands of high school pupils specimens of English prose that shall be eminently interesting to read and study in class, and which shall serve as models of clear and vigorous writing.

The subjects of the essays are such as to bring them into close relation with the study of general English literature.

The annotation is intended to serve as a guide and stimulus to research rather than as a substitute for research. The *notes*, therefore, are few in number. Only when an allusion of Macaulay is decidedly difficult to verify does the editor give the result of his own investigations. In all other cases he leads the pupil to make investigation for himself, believing that a good method in English, as in other studies, should leave as much free play as possible to the activity of the learner.

Historical Essays of Macaulay

Edited by SAMUEL THURBER. 12mo, cloth, 394 pages. Price, 80 cents.

THIS selection includes the essays on Lord Clive, Warren Hastings, and both those on the Earl of Chatham. The text in each case is given entire. A map of India, giving the location of places named in the essays, is included.

The notes are intended to help the pupil to help himself. They do not attempt to take the place of dictionary, encyclopædia, and such histories as are within the reach of ordinary students in academies or high schools. When an allusion is not easily understood, a note briefly explains it, or at least indicates where an explanation may be found. In other cases the pupil is expected to rely on his own efforts, and on such assistance as his teacher may think wise to give.

Select Essays of Addison

With Macaulay's Essay on Addison. Edited by SAMUEL THURBER, 12mo, 320 pages; cloth, 80 cents; boards, 50 cents.

THE purpose of this selection is to interest young students in Addison as a moral teacher, a painter of character, a humorist, and as a writer of elegant English. Hence the editor has aimed to bring together such papers from the *Spectator*, the *Tatler*, the *Guardian*, and the *Freeholder* as will prove most readable to youth of high school age, and at the same time give something like an adequate idea of the richness of Addison's vein. The De Coverley papers are of course all included. Papers describing eighteenth-century life and manners, especially such as best exhibit the writer in his mood of playful satire, have been drawn upon as peculiarly illustrating the Addisonian humor. The tales and allegories, as well as the graver moralizings, have due representation, and the beautiful *hymns* are all given.

Professor Henry S. Pancoast, *Philadelphia*: I am delighted to find that you are continuing the work so well begun in the Macaulay. I read the Introduction with much interest, and with a fresh sense of the importance and value of the method of teaching you are working to advance.

William C. Collar, *Principal of Latin School, Roxbury, Mass.*: I suppose the best thing I can say is that your book will go into our list of books to be read, and that it will have a permanent place in my school. I believe with all my heart in your principles of annotation, and think you are doing a great work for the schools.

Macaulay's Essays on Milton and Addison

12mo, boards. Price, 30 cents.

THESE are reprinted from Mr. Thurber's *Select Essays of Macaulay* and *Select Essays of Addison*, without any change in the numbering of the pages. Strongly and attractively bound, and printed on good paper, this book forms the cheapest and best edition of these two essays for school use.

Irving's Sketch-Book

With notes by Professor ELMER E. WENTWORTH, Vassar College. 12mo, cloth, 426 pages. Price, 60 cents.

THIS is the best and cheapest edition of the complete Sketch-Book now before the public. The paper and press-work are excellent, and the binding is strong and handsome. In his notes the editor has endeavored to stimulate, not supersede, thought on the part of the pupil, and so to prepare him to read with profit and enjoyment other literary masterpieces. What success has been attained in this direction may be estimated from the following extracts from letters recently received from those who have examined the book.

Professor Wm. Lyon Phelps, *New Haven, Conn.:* Please accept my thanks for your handsome edition of the Sketch-Book, which seems to me surprisingly cheap in price for such a book.

Professor Chas. F. Richardson, *Dartmouth College, Hanover, N.H.:* I thank you for sending me Mr. Wentworth's well-annotated edition of Irving's Sketch-Book, a pleasure to the eye and the hand, and sure to aid in the enjoyment of an American classic.

Professor Wm. H. Brown, *Johns Hopkins University :* I have to thank you for a copy of your very neat edition of Irving's classic Sketch-Book. I shall call the attention of my classes to it and its exceeding cheapness.

Irving H. Upton, *Principal of High School, Portsmouth, N.H.:* I examined it with a great deal of pleasure arising from two points in particular. First, from the remarkable execution of the book mechanically and typographically; and, secondly, because of the judicious absence of useless notes.

Professor T. W. Hunt, *Princeton College, N.J.:* Thanks for Wentworth's neat and convenient edition of the Sketch-Book. Had I seen it earlier, I should have inserted it in our catalogue for 1893-1894.

Professor Wm. E. Smyser, *De Pauw University, Greencastle, Ind.:* I am very much pleased with the book in every particular.

Professor Edward A. Allen, *University of Missouri, Columbia, Mo.:* Please accept my thanks for a copy of Wentworth's Irving's Sketch-Book, which strikes me as the best school edition I have seen.

Professor O. B. Clark, *Ripon College, Ripon, Wis.:* Permit me to congratulate you on the beauty of the volume, on its cheapness, and, above all, on the scholarly taste, modest reserve, and encouraging suggestiveness of the notes. Reading and study are made to beget reading and study, and the appetite will surely grow with what it feeds on.

www.ingramcontent.com/pod-product-compliance
Lightning Source LLC
Chambersburg PA
CBHW030407170426
43202CB00010B/1526